MW01515394

Voices from Heaven and Hell

by

J. MARCELLUS KIK

www.solidchristianbooks.com

2015

Contents

Preface

It was with trepidation some years ago that I gave a message in monologue form to my congregation in Montreal, Canada. It was well received and I was encouraged to give more. The series have been used both in Canada and United States in evangelistic services.

One encouraging feature was that the narratives attracted the attention of those who were difficult to reach with the conventional type sermon. It had its appeal also to young people and children.

It should be carefully noted in the narratives that the experience of death does not change an individual. It is a popular misconception that those in hell would accept the Gospel if it were offered to them. There is no repentance in hell. Death does not change character, as is so evident in the parable which our Lord gave concerning Dives and Lazarus. Death does not change the human heart nor does the torment of hell. Therefore the characters who speak from hell are kept "In character."

When the characters utter historical statements they have been taken from either sacred or secular history. They are not the product of the imagination but the result of research. We have sought especially to weave the revelation of Scripture into the voices from Heaven and hell. Thus they may be looked upon as character studies.

J.M.K.

Little Falls, N. J.

CHAPTER ONE "There Was No Room For Us In The Inn" by JOSEPH

"My name is Joseph. My father's name was Jacob and the name of my grandfather was Matthan. We were direct descendants of King David. This was a matter of pride both to my father and grandfather. They loved to tell me of the exploits of David and the prophecies of the future glory of our family. They read to me this prophecy of Jeremiah: '**Behold, the days come, saith the Lord, that I will raise unto David a righteous Branch, and a King shall reign and prosper, and shall execute judgment and justice in the earth. In his day Judah shall be saved, and Israel shall dwell safely: and this is his name whereby he shall be called, THE LORD OUR RIGHTEOUSNESS**.' My parents insisted that I learn all the prophecies which concerned the family David and it seemed to me that there were hundreds of them.

"It was hard to see how the Messiah would ever be born from our branch of the family of David. We were very poor. At one time we lived in Bethlehem, the city of David. Father found it such a struggle to live that he moved to Nazareth in order to better his condition. This move did not help us and we still remained poor. I learned the trade of carpenter. I discovered that the work was scarce and the wages poor.

"However, I was not sorry that we had moved to Nazareth. I fell in love with a young woman whose name was Mary. I need not tell you that I thought she was the most beautiful girl that I had ever met. Her goodness matched her beauty. I was constantly amazed at her knowledge of the Law and the Prophets. It was her special delight to memorize the Psalms of David. When I discovered that she loved me I was the proudest man in Israel.

"We became espoused one to another. According to our Hebrew law this meant that any violation of our vows would bring about punishment. In the sight of the law we were husband and wife although our actual marriage was not to take place for about a year. Both of us eagerly looked forward to the time of our marriage.

4

her encouragement and cheer. Then suddenly we beheld Bethlehem. It looked so peaceful and quiet.

"We hastened our steps and arrived in the court-yard of the Inn. The keeper of the Inn came out to us and before I could ask him for a room he said: "I am very sorry, sir, but there is no room in the Inn. If you had been a day earlier we might have provided for you. Every room is now taken.' This news stunned me and I said to him: "My wife is weary and sick. She is with child. We have traveled from Nazareth. Surely there is some room in which we could stay. It matters not how small.' But he answered: "Far be it for me to refuse room to a son of David. The trouble is that the Romans and the tax-collectors have taken every room.' He told me, too, that it was no use looking elsewhere in town for a room as a number of others had tried it without success. In puzzlement I asked him: "What are we to do? My wife is too sick to sleep in the cold night air.' To this the inn-keeper gave reply: 'I do not like to suggest it. But if you are agreeable to sleep in the stable we will turn out one of the beasts from its stall. We will put in some clean straw and make it as comfortable as possible.'

"Sick at heart I turned to Mary and said: "There is no room for us in the Inn or in the town. It breaks my heart to take you into a stable.' To this Mary replied: "Never mind, Joseph. GOD will take care of us. The stable will protect us from the wind. It will, at least, be warm. I am so cold and weary that any place will be welcome.'

"And during the night she brought forth her first-born son, and wrapped him in swaddling clothes, and laid him in a manger; because there was no room for us in the Inn. As we looked at the little babe our hearts thrilled and also a feeling of awe came over us. Here in a manger was He who would redeem Israel. We could hardly believe it.

"Not long after the birth of the child we heard the voices of men outside of the stable. We wondered who they were. At their knock I opened the door of the stable. They were shepherds. They asked me if it were true that a babe was born and was wrapped in swaddling clothes in a manger. In amazement I told them that was true and asked how they knew. One of the shepherds replied: '**We** were watching our flock in a field near Bethlehem. And, lo, the angel of the Lord came upon us, and the glory of the Lord shone round about us, and we were sore afraid. The angel said to us: Fear not: for, behold, I bring you good tidings of great joy, which shall be to all people. For unto you is born this day in the city of David a Saviour, which is Christ the Lord. And this shall be a sign unto you; ye shall find the babe wrapped in swaddling clothes, lying in a manger. And suddenly there was with the angel a multitude of the heavenly host praising God, and saying, Glory to God in the highest, and on earth peace, good will toward men**. When the angels disappeared out of our sight we hastened here to see this thing which the Lord had made known unto us. May we see Him who is CHRIST the Lord?'

"I led them to the manger where the babe was lying. The shepherds worshipped GOD and praised Him for the fulfillment of His promise to Israel. We did not lack visitors that day for the shepherds made known abroad the saying which was told them of the child. Later on I was fortunate to obtain a room in one of the homes in Bethlehem. After eight days the child was circumcised even according to our law. We followed the instructions of the angel and called his name JESUS. This name in our Hebrew tongue means *Jehovah is salvation.*

"Forty days after the blessed event Mary and I traveled with the child to the Temple at Jerusalem that Mary might be purified according to the law of Moses and that we might present the child to the Lord. It was the law that every firstborn male belonged to GOD. In our presentation we sacrificed to the Lord two young pigeons. We were too poor to offer a yearling lamb. Our GOD is gracious in allowing the poor to substitute young pigeons.

"At the Temple an old man by the name of Simeon took the infant JESUS into his arms. Then he said: '**Lord, now lettest thou thy servant depart in peace, according to thy word: for mine eyes have seen thy salvation, which thou hast prepared before the face of all people; a light to lighten the Gentiles, and the glory of thy people Israel**.' And while Mary and I marveled at this saying Simeon turned to Mary and said: '**Behold, this child is set for the fall and rising again of many in Israel; and for a sign which**

shall be spoken against; (Yea, a sword shall pierce through thy own soul also,) that the thoughts of many hearts may be revealed.' This saying mystified us.

"We returned to Bethlehem where several other events awaited us. We had scarcely settled when strange and foreign men appeared. They were Magi from the East. They asked me if they might see the child that was born to be King of the Jews. I invited them into the house. When they saw the child they fell down and worshipped him. They opened their treasures and presented unto him gifts; gold, and frankincense, and myrrh. Afterwards they told us their experience. They had seen the star in the East. They told us how Herod at Jerusalem had informed them that the Messiah was to be born in Bethlehem and how they had seen the star again. Then they left us to stay at the Inn.

"That night the angel of the Lord appeared to me again. He said: '**Arise and take the young child and his mother, and flee into Egypt, and be thou there until I bring thee word; for Herod will seek the young child to destroy him**: We left Bethlehem immediately and journeyed into Egypt. GOD had made provision for us through the gold which the Magi presented. We were not happy in Egypt and rejoiced greatly when the angel appeared again to me in a dream. He said: '**Arise, and take the young child and his mother, and go into the land of Israel; for they are dead which sought the young child's life**.'

"We entered into the land of Israel but when I heard that Archelaus did reign in Judea in the place of his father Herod, I was afraid to dwell in Bethlehem. So we traveled to Nazareth where I gained employment as a carpenter. And there we brought up the child JESUS.

"I never dreamed that life would be so full when I took Mary for wife. The Lord was gracious to his humble servant. Of all the events, what stands out the most, is the fact that there was no room for us in the Inn. The Messiah was born in a stable. At the time that pained my heart. But would it not be terrible if there were no room in the hearts of men for the Saviour which is CHRIST the

Lord? There would be no salvation from sin. May the words of the angel be fulfilled to the Israel of GOD:

'He shall save his people from their sins.'"

CHAPTER TWO "I Heard The Carol Of The Angels" by A Judean Shepherd

"I was one of the shepherds keeping watch over the Temple flock near to Bethlehem. It still mystifies me that my fellow shepherds and I were chosen to hear the first announcement of the birth of the Messiah. We were poor and despised by many. Nevertheless we heard the carol of the angels. Let me tell you of our experience.

"The Temple in Jerusalem required many lambs and sheep for the sacrificial service. A number of flocks were maintained for the provision of these sacrifices. Ours was one of them. Along with two friends I took care of the flock that was near Bethlehem. My name is Reuben and the names of the other two shepherds are Thomas and Caleb. This particular night Thomas and I were sitting near a fire while Caleb was making the rounds. It was very cold that night and we enjoyed the warm fire.

"Thomas asked me if I did not think that Caleb was taking rather long in making the rounds. He was taking long and I was a little worried for fear that he was having trouble. This led us to talk about Caleb. Thomas felt that he was rather peculiar and that he had strange views of the Messiah. He told me that Caleb did not agree at all with the views of our Rabbi Annas of the synagogue we attended.

"Of course, Thomas did not know Caleb as well as I did. I knew his background. He had attended the school of the rabbis in Jerusalem. Something happened and he did not become a rabbi. He became a shepherd like his father. He continued to study the Law and the Prophets. This I related to Thomas. He, however, still mistrusted Caleb because he did not follow all the traditions of the elders.

"While we were discussing him we saw him coming in the distance. The stars were very bright that night. As he approached we saw that he was carrying one of the flock. It was a little lamb. Apparently it had been mauled by a wolf. He told us what happened and how he was able to save this lamb and scare away the wolves. We all hated these wolves. Talking about wolves led Thomas to speak about his pet hate which was Herod whom he called a blood-thirsty wolf. And he surely is a wolf. He put to death his own wife and mother-in-law. His hands were dripping with the blood of those he murdered. Would that we could protect Israel from Herod as we protected the flock from marauding beasts. But, as Caleb mentioned, only GOD could be such a Shepherd. Some day the great Shepherd of the flock will avenge the ill-treatment of Israel.

"Talking about Herod caused us to talk about taxes. It was Herod's purpose to bleed us to death with taxes in order that he might send large sums to Rome. He wanted to stand in good favour with the Emperor. Just recently the Emperor had made a decree that all the world was to be taxed. And you can well believe that Herod would see that we paid our share. For this tax we had to enroll in the village or town of our family. That is why the town of Bethlehem was filled with strangers. It was a shame that all of the lineage of David had to travel from afar just for the privilege of enrolling for more taxes. Some had to come from as far as Nazareth. 'Tis said that the Inn was crowded and there was no more room. What some of the travelers will do is beyond me. And all because the Romans want to increase our taxes. Would that GOD would send the Messiah to deliver us from Herod and the Romans. Thomas asked me whether I thought the Messiah would appear in our day.

"It so happened that I heard Rabbi Annas teach on that subject on the previous Sabbath. I told the men what I heard. It seems according to the figures of some Rabbis that the Messiah should soon appear. It was the opinion of some that the Messiah would come 4,000 years after the creation.

Others place the time 4,291 years after the creation. Some of the Rabbis maintained that the Messiah would come when the world is thoroughly wicked. I told the men that it was the personal opinion of Rabbi Annas that the Messiah would come when all within our nation are righteous. He seemed to think that such a day would soon arrive as he thought most Israelites were righteous except such shepherds as we because we did not have time to fulfill all the rituals of the law. Knowing that Caleb was learned in these things, I asked him what his opinion was.

"He replied: 'The Scriptures do not tell us the exact time, Reuben. GOD will send the Messiah in the fulness of time. As to waiting for Israel to become righteous it seems to me that Rabbi Annas is wrong. Israel is becoming very wicked. Jerusalem is a city of iniquity. I dare not tell you of the wickedness I observed while studying in the school of the rabbis. Even the priests are living immoral lives. Their greed is polluting the worship of the Temple. There was a time when I rejoiced to be a shepherd of the Temple flock. All these sheep before us and the lambs will be used to obtain the forgiveness of sins by offering them upon the altar. And to know that I have a part in taking care of the flock so that they will be without blemish used to thrill me. But the priests are using these sheep for their own profit and are selling them even within the Temple. Just the other day they even sold a pair of pigeons for a gold denar. And they had just paid a few pence for it. When the Temple is so desecrated Israel is not so righteous. I used to think that the Messiah would come when the children of Israel would repent. But they are far from repentance.

Now I believe with all my heart that the Messiah will come when the mercy of GOD decrees it. His coming depends entirely upon GOD's will and mercy.'

"We discussed this point for a while and then we entered into a discussion as to what the Messiah would do when He came. Thomas and I felt that one of the first things He would do would be to establish the Kingdom and vanquish Herod and the Romans. Caleb quoted a passage from the prophet Jeremiah which stated: '**Behold, the days come, saith the Lord, that I will raise unto David a righteous Branch, and a King shall reign and prosper, and shall execute judgment and justice in the earth**.' We were delighted to hear that quotation from the prophet. The Messiah would be a great King and execute judgment against the Romans. We hoped that He would tax them to death.

"Caleb halted us from such thoughts of revenge. He said that the Messiah would reign with love and righteousness. And if we were to reign with Him we would have to change. We could not be like the Romans. We could not be cruel and selfish like Herod. Well, that would mean that we would have to possess new hearts for I still could not see how it would be possible to have love towards the Romans. I hated them.

"Then Caleb expressed a thought about the Messiah which I never heard before. I am sure that Rabbi Annas never expressed it in my hearing. Caleb said that the greatest task of the Messiah would be to save His people from their sins. Thomas asked him how the Messiah could do that. Caleb said that he wasn't quite sure. But he had been studying the prophet Isaiah of late. The prophet indicated that GOD would lay on the Messiah the iniquity of His people. Caleb declared that Isaiah had also written that the Servant of the Lord would be wounded for our transgressions and bruised for our iniquities. He said to Thomas that he would rather have his sins forgiven than to tax the Romans a thousand golden talents.

"Both Thomas and I felt a little guilty. I suppose we should not imitate the wicked Romans. I confessed that I, too, was concerned with my sins. I know that I am guilty before GOD. The Psalmists and the Prophets declare that GOD will punish sin. I said to Thomas: 'To have peace with GOD would give more joy than to tax the Romans and even Herod.' Thomas admitted that he was also concerned about his sins. He longed to be reconciled to GOD. But neither he nor I looked upon the Messiah in that light. We looked upon Him as a King who would deliver us from Herod and the Romans. It would indeed be wonderful if He would deliver us from sin. That would be a greater deliverance. We encouraged Caleb to tell us more of the teachings of the Scriptures.

"Caleb could not tell us much more. He pointed out that Moses had indicated that the Messiah would teach us as He would be a greater prophet than Moses. What a wonderful person the Messiah would be. He would not only be a greater prophet than Moses but He would be a greater king than David and a greater priest than Aaron. Glorious would be His coming. I suppose that if He came in our day we shepherds would not see Him. The Messiah would be surrounded by the chief priests, the scribes, the Pharisees, and the rulers. However, that did not matter. The important thing was His coming. And I said to the others that if He came in our day I would leave the flock and travel to Jerusalem for just a glimpse of Him.

"Caleb then surprised us again with his knowledge of the Scriptures. He said that the prophet Micah had written that the Messiah would be born in Bethlehem. I could hardly believe that. There is no dwelling in Bethlehem that is fit for Him. The grandest place was the Inn. And surely that would not be good enough for the King to have as His birthplace. Yet that was the declaration of Micah.

"As we talked about Bethlehem we glanced in the direction of the city of David. We could see it so clearly. It seemed to lie so still and peaceful. Never has it been so light. The light seemed almost supernatural. It was supernatural! It was a heavenly light! Something mysterious was happening.

"**And, lo, the angel of the Lord came upon us, and the glory of the Lord shone round about us: and we were sore afraid. And the angel said unto us: 'Fear not: for behold, I bring you good tidings of great joy which shall be to all people. For unto you is born this day in the city of David a Saviour, which is Christ the Lord. And this shall be a sign unto you; ye shall find the babe wrapped in swaddling clothes, lying in a manger.' And suddenly there was with the angel a multitude of heavenly host praising God and saying, 'Glory to God in the highest, and on earth peace, good will toward men.'**

"And it came to pass, as the angels were gone away from us into Heaven, that we said one to another: '**Let us now go even unto Bethlehem, and see this thing which is come to pass which the Lord hath made known unto us.**' We actually ran to Bethlehem. The angel said that we would find the babe in a manger. We determined to go first to the stable of the Inn. It was hard to conceive that the Messiah would be born in a stable; nevertheless there is where we went.

"I shall never forget the startled look on the face of young Joseph and Mary his wife. They wondered who had informed us of the birth of the child and who had directed us to the stable. With great pride Mary showed us the little babe lying in the manger. It was wrapped in swaddling clothes. This was the sign of which the angel spake. We accepted the word of the angel that this babe was Messiah the Lord. In quiet reverence we worshipped Him. We related to Mary and Joseph the words of the angel and told them the carol of the angels.

"We then spread the news throughout Bethlehem. All wondered at the words of the angel and the carol of the heavenly host. After telling all our friends we returned to the flock. How we glorified and praised GOD! The day of deliverance was at hand. He is born that will redeem Israel. '**Glory to God in the highest and on earth peace, and good will among men**.' "

CHAPTER THREE "I Beheld His Star" by Balthasar

"Light came to me through a beautiful star. Darkness was my lot. It was the darkness of ignorance and the darkness of superstition. But a marvellous light shattered that darkness. A star of hope brought me to Him who is the Light of the world. Wonderful is the mercy of the GOD of the world who manifested that light to those who were dwelling in darkness.

"I belonged to the priestly caste of the Magi. My name is Balthasar. In the darkness of ignorance I was a follower of Zoroaster. I kept the sacred fires and made sacrifices to Ahura Mazda whom we worshipped as the god of creation. We also worshipped the elements: fire, air, earth, and water. We felt that there was a struggle between the universal spirit of good and the universal spirit of evil. We took a part in that struggle by killing with our own hands the animals which were of the bad creation: such as, snakes, harmful insects, and birds of prey. Our special worship was that of fire. No doubt, this was due to our groping after light. Also we were students of the stars which we felt had an influence on the lives of men. As Magi we interpreted dreams and had the gift of prophecy. But in spite of our worship of light we were in terrible darkness.

"During my career as a priest I became very dissatisfied. It seemed as though we were waging a losing battle. I could kill the wicked creatures of the evil creation but I could not kill the evil of my own heart and that of my fellowmen. We lived not only in the darkness of ignorance and the darkness of superstition but in the darkness of misery. Poverty, strife, and wickedness surrounded us. It seemed that the evil spirit was in complete control.

"There came upon me an intense longing for a deliverer and for a golden age of happiness and peace. I felt that the religion of Zoroaster would not bring this to pass. It was then that I came in contact with a descendant of the Jews who had long ago been taken captive by Sargon the great King. Not all the Jews had

According to Belteshazzar this kingdom would never be destroyed. It was to be an everlasting kingdom. Melchior felt that this would benefit all the earth and he longed for the fulfillment of the prophecy of Belteshazzar. GOD revealed to him, also, that a star would signalize the birth of this King. So happy was he when he beheld it that he determined to travel to the country of the Jews.

"The wonderful providence of GOD led our paths to cross and we determined to travel together. It was indeed thrilling when we beheld the walls of Jerusalem the chief city of the Jews. It was beautiful for situation. No doubt the citizens of Jerusalem would still be celebrating the birth of the promised King. When we entered in by the gates we asked: '**Where is He that is born King of the Jews? For we saw His star in the East, and are come to worship Him**.'

"We were dumbfounded by the reception our question received. The first group we asked refused to answer and seemed troubled. They repeated the question to others. As a result a great crowd of people gathered about us. They were quite excited as they talked among themselves. Although we asked several no one would answer our question. We were puzzled. Then an officer of King Herod approached and asked us to follow him to Herod. To our amazement Herod frowned and seemed displeased when we asked him where the newborn King was so that we could worship Him. He asked us to wait so that he could consult the chief priests and scribes who were the Jewish Magi.

"After consulting them, King Herod called us privately. He said that according to one of the prophets of the Jews the King was to be born in Bethlehem of Judea. He quoted the prophecy as it had been given to him: '**And thou Bethlehem, in the land of Juda, art not the least among the princes of Juda: for out of thee shall come a Governor, that shall rule my people Israel**:' You would almost think that Herod was reading his death sentence so black was his countenance. But we were mistaken for he said: '**Go and search diligently for the young child; and when ye have found him, bring me word again, that I may come and worship him also**:' This delighted us and we went our way.

"All this had taken so much time that it was dark when we started. To our joy the star, which we beheld in the East, appeared again. It guided us and stood over the place where the young child was. We were invited into the house and saw the young child with Mary His mother. At last we were able to worship Him whom Isaiah declared was the Prince of Peace; whom Balaam had declared would be a Star out of Jacob; and whom Belteshazzar had declared would be Ruler over all people, nations, and languages.

"We had not come empty-handed. We desired to present gifts worthy of such a King. Anything less than gold would be unworthy to present to Him who would rule the world. We also had precious ointments, frankincense and myrrh. These precious ointments were given by many only to gods. But surely this child is the Son of GOD. With our gifts we acknowledged Him to be our Ruler and GOD.

"Joseph and Mary told us of the events which had occurred previous to our visit. They told us of the messages which they had received from the angel of GOD. They told us about the shepherds and the carol the angels sang to them. They told us more about the Messiah who was prophesied in the writings of the prophets. We became all the more convinced that the Child was indeed the King of kings and the Ruler over the nations.

"It was late when we retired to the Inn. Our hearts were filled with joy and praise. During the night the Lord revealed to us in a dream that we should not return to Herod. This showed that we were not mistaken about Herod. He was displeased with the news of the birth of this Child. But we were overjoyed. We returned to our land with the news of the birth of Him who would conquer evil and establish righteousness.

"With the revelation of the star the darkness of ignorance and the darkness of superstition were vanquished. The star led us to Him who is the Light of the world. As the Light of the King vanquished the darkness in our souls so may He vanquish the darkness among all people of the world."

CHAPTER FOUR "I held the Saviour In My Arms" by SIMEON

"My name is Simeon. For almost a century I have lived in the city of Jerusalem. During the years of my pilgrimage many sad days have been witnessed by my eyes. But now all is forgotten for I have seen the consolation of Israel. My eyes have seen the Messiah so long promised to Israel. But before telling you what my eyes have seen may I give you some of my history and that of Jerusalem.

"I am an Israelite. Of my birth I have full reason to be proud. I belong to a chosen race and a chosen nation. Of all the nations of the world Israel was chosen of GOD to be His peculiar people. It is an honour and privilege to belong to the Jewish race. I mention this because I must mention some things which are not complimentary to my race. It is with shame and bowed head that I must tell you of the degradation of my race and particularly of the citizens of the Holy City, Jerusalem. But do not forget that it is my race that brought forth Abraham, Isaac and Jacob. It is my race that brought forth Moses. It is my race that brought forth King David and King

Solomon. It is my race that brought forth a royal line of prophets like Daniel, Isaiah, Jeremiah, Ezekiel and others. They shone like the stars of the firmament. And it is Israel that brought forth the Messiah, the Saviour of the world. Do not forget the light as I tell you of the darkness.

"Because of the unfaithfulness of my people to the living GOD, Israel has been subject to many Gentile powers. Three hundred years ago Alexander the Great conquered our country and we were subjects of the Grecian Empire. But soon thereafter we became subject to Egypt under the Ptolemies under whom we suffered greatly. One hundred and twenty-two years later we were released from Egypt by the Syrian Antiochus. He tried to impose his pagan idolatries upon my people. GOD sent us the Maccabees who led Israel in revolt against heathen tyranny some 166 years ago. But, alas, under our own rulers there occurred civil war after civil war.

There was no rest nor peace in Israel. Some 63 years ago, and I remember it well, the Roman General Pompey attacked Jerusalem on the Sabbath day while many of us were at worship. Many of my countrymen and friends were slain at the altar of worship. From that time until now we have been subject to Rome.

"Some forty years ago the Idumean, Herod, was appointed King over Judea by the Romans. No words of mine can adequately describe the cruelty and bestiality of this monster Herod. He is not a Jew, nor a Greek, nor a Roman. He is an Idumean, a barbarian. By bribery and treachery he obtained his throne. His hands are dripping with the blood of his own wife and her mother. He had his own sons strangled to death. Many an Israelite he has put to death just upon a whim. It was his delight to see them burning alive.

"Why did GOD allow such a monster to occupy the throne of David? Alas, it was because of the sins of my people. My people are religious but their religion is a sham. For every Israelite without guile there are a hundred who are hypocrites. The priests are intent on the making of money and mark up even the temple sacrificial animals for gain. The Pharisees are so selfrighteous. You see them on the street corners making long prayers. They go through the forms of religion but there is no mercy or love in their hearts. They broaden their phylacteries but the law is not in their hearts. They make prey of the poor and widows.

"The morality of my people in Jerusalem is such that one can only hang his head in shame as he speaks of it. Drunkenness is rife even on the holy days. Indecent dress degrades the daughters of Zion. Even high priestly youths are dressed indecently. Adultery is common amongst the high and low. It is a sad day indeed when Israelites ape the Gentile Greeks and Romans in morals and manners. This is Jerusalem of today.

"In the midst of all this darkness of immorality, hypocrisy, and political oppression there shone one star of hope in my heart and that was the coming of the promised Messiah. But what would my people do to the Messiah if He came? The thought often frightens me. As I stand here in the Temple I cannot help thinking what that priest would do who is intent on cheating his fellow countrymen in

" 'The Lord bless thee, and keep thee: the Lord make His face to shine upon thee, and be gracious unto thee: the Lord lift up His countenance upon thee, and give thee peace. Amen.' "

CHAPTER FIVE "The Scriptures Are Not Sufficient" by Dives

"I am known as Dives although that is not my real name. Through no great fault of my own I am a dweller in hell. There are those who speak of suffering hell upon earth as though any torment upon earth can compare to the torment of hell. They do not know what they are speaking about. No torment upon earth is unending. There is always some break such as sleep. There is always some one on hand to help or comfort. But torment in hell is unending. It is day and night. It can best be compared to being in a flame of fire. This burning flame of fire cannot be extinguished. There is no pause. There is no rest. There is no comfort. It is anguish, anguish, anguish; suffering, suffering, suffering; torment, torment, torment.

"Do I deserve this endless anguish, this everlasting suffering, this eternal torment? Let me tell you my story and you can judge for yourself.

"While upon earth I was respected in my community. Although I did not attend the synagogue as faithfully as I should nevertheless I was not irreligious. During the Passover I went through all the required ritual. The prominent Rabbis, Scribes, and Priests respected me.

"I was a man of extreme wealth. It was through my own efforts and ingenuity that I became rich. After the accumulation of wealth I retired from business in order to enjoy life. I had more money than I could possibly spend so why not enjoy it? Why not eat, drink, and be merry if one has the means to do so? There were only a few in my town who could afford to dress in purple and fine linen. The purple was the garment of royalty. The fine linen which I wore daily was imported from Egypt. Its glory was its dazzling whiteness. For much of this I had to pay its weight in gold. There were few who could afford to dress as I did.

"My friends and I dined sumptuously every day. My banquets were the talk of the town. I was not satisfied with the food which

Palestine could supply but imported delicacies from other nations. The world-famous wines of Lebanon were plentiful at my table. I spared no expense and my tables literally groaned under the weight of food. We did eat, drink, and were merry.

"There is always a fly in the ointment. The fly in the ointment of my enjoyment was a beggar by the name of Lazarus. During a banquet one of my servants called my attention to the fact that Lazarus was lying at the gates of my mansion and desired food. I knew something about this beggar. He had some disease which prevented him from working. If he had been as diligent as I was he would not have been reduced to this position for he would have saved enough to keep him during his sickness and old age. I have no sympathy for men who do not provide for their future.

"I had heard that he was a deeply religious man. His name indicated that. It means '*GOD is my trust.*' All the good his trust in GOD did him! For all his prayers and devotions he was nothing but a diseased beggar. It just goes to show that such religious fanaticism does not pay. It makes one no richer and now this religious Lazarus was, bothering me for food from my table.

"I rose up and went to the porch to observe this beggar who had come to annoy me in the midst of our merriment. He was a filthy sight. He had sores all over his body. Some dogs were standing: by him. They licked his sores as though they would heal him with their tongues. That picture often torments my mind. Lazarus had dogs, at least to comfort him and to moisten his fevered body with their cool tongues.

"But to me it was a revolting sight and I hastened back to the banquet hall to forget this beggar. One of my servants asked if he should carry out food to the beggar. I said, 'No.' Then this servant had the impudence to suggest that perhaps I could spare some of the crumbs which had fallen upon the floor. I replied that not one crumb would I give to Lazarus. 'But the beggar is starving,' insisted this servant. 'It matters not to me,' I replied. 'That is his concern. Besides he has great confidence in GOD. Let GOD help him. I do not want to hear about this beggar any more. Tell the musicians to play. This is a time for merriment and not for thinking about diseased beggars.'

"They told me the following day that Lazarus had died. 'Good riddance!' was my thought. 'The sooner that type die the better. They are a disgrace to the community.' They dragged him to a field and buried him in a few feet of ground. Even the Rabbis did not consider him important enough to give him a proper funeral.

"It was not long after this that I took ill. Four physicians attended me. They did everything humanly possible to heal me. But nothing seemed to help. I did not want to die for I hated to leave all my possessions. However, I was not afraid to die. I was a Jew and a descendant of Abraham. My Rabbi had told me that all the children of Abraham would enter into Heaven. Besides I had lived a good life. I was a respected citizen and had made my mark in the community. Why then should I be afraid to die? I lived as good and perhaps better than most people. I had committed no crimes.

"I died and I awakened in hell. I lifted my eyes and afar off I beheld Abraham with Lazarus in his bosom. I cried out; '**Father Abraham, have mercy on me, and send Lazarus, that he may dip the tip of his finger in water, and cool my tongue; for I am tormented in this flame**.' I called Abraham '**father**' to remind him of my claim on him. Was I not his descendant and as such deserving of his mercy and favour? If I could be successful in obtaining the least favour on the ground of his fatherhood it would not be difficult to obtain greater favours. The favour I asked was indeed small. I did not ask for a cup of water. I did not ask for as much as could be carried in the palm of his hand. I did not ask for so much as a drop of water. All I asked was that he might dip the tip of his finger in water and cool my burning tongue. Just to feel moisture on my tongue for a moment would bring such relief and would strengthen my claim on Abraham.

"But, alas, Abraham did not grant my request. He said; '**Son, remember that thou in thy lifetime receivedst thy good things, and likewise Lazarus evil things: but now he is comforted, and thou art tormented. And besides all this, between us and you there is a great gulf fixed; so that they which would pass from**

31

hence to you cannot; neither can they pass to us that would come from thence.'

"He acknowledged my physical descent from him but not that I was a genuine son entitled to all the promises. My strategy did not work. And reminding me of the good things which I enjoyed upon earth! The very remembrance of them torments my mind and soul. It makes hell even worse. And how was I to know that there was an impassable gulf between hell and Heaven? How was I to know that there was not another opportunity to gain Heaven in the life after death? How was I to know that I would be placed in hell and abide there forever? It is not fair. There was nothing upon earth to warn me. If GOD were a GOD of mercy why did He not send a special message of warning? Ah, that is it! It is GOD's fault. I will call that to the attention of Abraham.

"So I called to Abraham and said: '**I pray thee therefore, father, that thou wouldest send him to my father's house; for I have five brethren; that he may testify unto them, lest they also come into this place of torment**.' Yes, if Abraham would send Lazarus to my five brothers with a message of warning, it would be sufficient to warn them. They knew Lazarus for they were present at the banquet when I refused to send out food to feed him. If he were to come to them risen from the dead they would believe him. He could tell them to place their trust and faith in GOD and to turn away from their sins. He could tell them what a terrible place hell is. He could tell them of the endless torment, suffering, and anguish. He could tell them about the beauty of Heaven and the eternal happiness of all those who are the true children of Abraham. Ah, if GOD had only sent Lazarus with such a testimony to me, I would have repented and placed my confidence in GOD rather than in my wealth. GOD did not warn me sufficiently. So let Lazarus now testify to my five brothers.

"Alas, Abraham did not heed my plea. He failed to see that I was not sufficiently warned. He sternly said to me; '**They have Moses and the prophets; let them hear them**.' I suppose he meant that I should have listened to Moses and the prophets while I was upon earth. In my generation there were few who took Moses and the prophets seriously. We were too busy. There was too much to

32

occupy our time. There were those like Lazarus who liked that sort of thing. But all my associates were busy getting and spending.

"Of course, I remember some of the teachings of Moses. From a child I was taught the law and the prophets. It was through Moses that we received the ten commandments. The sum of the second tablet of the law was that we should love our neighbour as ourselves. Who could keep such a law? That would mean that I would have to feed every beggar that came along. That would not be possible. And Moses said that the only way we could live in the favour of GOD was to keep that law. Otherwise the wrath of GOD would abide upon us. But surely GOD should realize that we could not keep such a law.

"It is true that some of the prophets gave messages of warning. They told us to worship the living GOD more than silver and gold. Some of them were dismal prophets. I remember this was especially true of Jeremiah. He was so pessimistic.

One young Rabbi read from his prophecy for several sabbaths. I asked him if he could not find pleasanter reading and that if he persisted in reading from Jeremiah I would stay home and cut off my contributions. He soon stopped.

"There were other prophets of woe and judgment. There was Hosea who warned that sin would reap retribution. There was Joel who told us to rend our hearts rather than our garments. Amos, Micah, Zephaniah and others spoke of the judgment of GOD against sin. But no one took their messages too seriously. It was all right for their day but it had no application for our days. I know that my five brothers, even as I, would not consider their messages sufficient to turn them from their sins to the worship of GOD. Abraham was wrong. Moses and the prophets were not sufficient to cause one to repent. I told him so. I said: '**Nay, father Abraham; but if one went from the dead unto them, they will repent**:'

"Ah yes, my brothers needed one who had risen from the dead. I know that if Lazarus had appeared to me after he died I would have believed him instantly. I would have repented of all my sins and lived a truly religious life. Father Abraham was wrong. But all that he said was: '**If they hear not Moses and the prophets, neither will they be persuaded though one rose from the dead.**'

"I tell you Abraham was wrong. The Scriptures are not sufficient to convince one of the reality of hell and of the punishment one will receive for sin. Moses and the prophets are not enough. We should have heard from one risen from the dead and then we would have repented. I tell you it was no fault of my own that I did not repent. It is not my fault that I am in this flame of fire. It is GOD's fault. It is His responsibility. I do not deserve unending anguish. I do not deserve everlasting suffering. I do not deserve eternal torment. Surely, surely, surely you will agree that Moses and the prophets are not sufficient guides of the life after death. The Scriptures are not sufficient."

CHAPTER SIX "I Was Born A Second Time" by Nicodemus

"My name is Nicodemus. It is my desire to give you my amazing experience with JESUS who is the Messiah. Of part of my experience I am thoroughly ashamed. But I trust that you will forgive me even as the living GOD has forgiven. I confess that I was a coward and a weakling. I was more afraid of the opinion of men than of GOD. But now all has changed. I was born a second time. Let me tell you of my experience.

"I am a Jew. I was a Pharisee. This is the strictest party of our nation. As a Pharisee I was very zealous of keeping the law of Moses and the traditions which we received from the elders. My father was a man of considerable wealth and was very anxious that I would become a teacher of the law. From early youth I attended the best schools in Jerusalem and sat at the feet of the famous rabbis of the day. The teachings of Moses, of Isaiah, of Daniel and the other prophets became my delight. The thousands of traditions which arose during the past centuries, too, were learned by heart. It was a proud day when I was accepted as a teacher of the law.

"As a Pharisee I was very zealous of the honour of my nation. The Romans who ruled Palestine were hated by all faithful Jews. We all longed for the day when a Deliverer would come who would release us from our bondage to the Gentiles whom we considered to be worse than dogs. We all looked for the coming of the Messiah who had been promised of GOD. We believed that He would set up a kingdom which would rule all the kingdoms of this world.

"Often Joseph of Arimathea, a close friend of mine, and I would speak of that day when we as Jews would rule the world even as the Romans were ruling. We spoke of the prophecies which indicated that the Messiah would change the hearts of the Gentiles so that they would leave their abominable practice of worshipping idols. The Jewish nation would be glorified in that day.

"I must confess that there was much within my nation which disturbed me. Many had no regard for the law. The significance of the sacrifices of the Temple was not known to many. Worship was a matter of form. The life of some of my friends was shocking. Even my associates in the Sanhedrin were wicked, cruel, and greedy. I had been honoured in being chosen to be ruler in the highest court of our nation, the Sanhedrin. I came to the court with high ideals of justice but these ideals were not shared by all.

"It was no wonder that some of us were greatly disturbed by the preaching of a man who was called John the Baptist. To us he seemed wild and uncouth. He had not attended the schools of the Rabbis. But the multitude flocked to hear him preach. Some of us went to hear him from Jerusalem. I can still remember his message which seared into my conscience. When he saw us he cried out: '**O generation of vipers, who hath warned you to flee from the wrath to come? Bring forth therefore fruits meet for repentance: and think not to say within yourselves, We have Abraham to our father: for I say unto you, that God is able of these stones to raise up children unto Abraham**.'

"This message enraged us. Surely he did not have to call us vipers. And why would not our descent from Abraham entitle us to the blessings of GOD? As long as we kept the law faithfully GOD would be pleased with us. And as the children of Abraham we would have the chief positions in the kingdom which the Messiah would set up. We were offended by the preaching of this John the Baptist. But he was such a powerful preacher and had such influence with the people that we could not help wondering if he might be the Messiah. When we asked him he denied this and said that he was sent to prepare the way for the Messiah. He claimed that the Messiah would come soon. However, as many had declared this previously we did not take him seriously.

"Not long after this I began to hear rumors about a man by the name of JESUS. He was a worker of miracles. At first in common with my friends I doubted the miracles were genuine. But I checked them. I personally interviewed a leper who had been cleansed; a man who had received sight; and a man who had been afflicted with palsy. There was no doubt in my mind that they were genuine

36

miracles. Now these miracles could be performed only by the power of GOD. This JESUS must be a prophet.

"I talked this matter over with some of my associates of the Sanhedrin. They were still feeling bitter about what John the Baptist had said and they classified this JESUS with him. They felt that his miraculous power came from Beelzebub, the prince of devils. It was their opinion that the multitude should be warned about him. Only the very ignorant would follow him.

"However, I was not satisfied with their opinion for I felt that no man could do such miracles except through the power of Almighty GOD. Of course, I did not want to antagonize my friends by telling them what I felt. They would consider me ignorant and I would lose their respect. I valued their opinion. But I could not deny the fact that this JESUS was a prophet of GOD. It disturbed me. I dared not listen to Him when He taught in Jerusalem. Some might think that I was His follower.

"One night I could not sleep and the thought struck me that I could see this JESUS without any one knowing anything about it. I found where He was lodging and He was awake. I asked if I could see Him in private. He consented. I said to Him, '**Rabbi, we know that thou art a teacher come from God: for no man can do these miracles that thou doest, except God be with him**.' To this He gave a strange reply: '**Verily, verily, I say unto thee, except a man be born again, he cannot see the Kingdom of God!**'

"What did He mean? That I, a Pharisee and a ruler of the Jews, would have to be born a second time? Did He mean that as a son of Abraham I was not entitled to be a citizen of the Kingdom of GOD? Had I not kept the law and traditions zealously? Surely He could not mean that I was not fit to enter into the Kingdom! But could He mean a physical rebirth? In my puzzlement I asked Him; '**How can a man be born when he is old? Can he enter the second time into his mother's womb, and be born?**'

"To this JESUS answered: '**Verily, verily, I say unto thee, Except a man be born of water and of the Spirit, he cannot enter into the Kingdom of God. That which is born of the flesh is flesh;**

and that which is born of the Spirit is spirit.' I knew by this that JESUS meant a spiritual rebirth. But why would it be necessary for me a Jew and a zealous keeper of the law to experience a spiritual rebirth? What was wrong with me? I was not conscious of any wrongdoing. If I had been a Sadducee or a Publican I could understand the necessity of repentance and spiritual rebirth. But from my youth I had been faithful to the law and the traditions. I had been honoured as a teacher of the law and a member of the Sanhedrin. Yet now this JESUS was telling me that it was necessary for me to experience repentance and a spiritual rebirth.

"The astonishment which I felt must have been written on my countenance for JESUS said: '**Marvel not that I say unto thee, Ye must be born again. The wind bloweth where it listeth, and thou hearest the sound thereof, but canst not tell whence it cometh, and whither it goeth; so is everyone that is born of the Spirit**.' This statement added to my bewilderment. For it seemed that this rebirth depended upon the Spirit of GOD. Did this JESUS not realize who I was? Did He not know my zeal for the law? Did not the fact that I was a Jew automatically make me fit for the Kingdom? So in my bewilderment I cried out: '**How can these things be?**'

"To this JESUS replied: '**Art thou a master of Israel, and knowest not these things ? Verily, verily, I say unto thee, we speak that we do know, and testify that we have seen; and ye receive not our witness. If I have told you earthly things, and ye believe not, how shall ye believe if I tell you of heavenly things? And no man hath ascended up to Heaven, but he that came down from Heaven, even the Son of man which is in Heaven**.'

"I knew by this reply that JESUS considered Himself to be the Messiah. It was Daniel who termed the Messiah: '**The Son of man**.' Was this JESUS the Son of man? Was He the Messiah? Was He the one who would set up the everlasting Kingdom? Was He the one who would deliver us from bondage to the Romans? Surely that could not be. He did not seem like a warrior. I could not picture this meek and mild man leading an army in bloody conflict. A prophet, yes; but not a king. Surely He could not be the Messiah.

"While these thoughts were disturbing my mind this JESUS made another startling statement which confused me more than ever. He said: '**And as Moses lifted up the serpent in the wilderness, even so must the Son of man be lifted up that whosoever believeth in Him should not perish, but have eternal life.**'

"The Son of man be lifted up as Moses lifted up the serpent in the wilderness? The Messiah nailed to a post? The thought shocked me. Many times had I taught this scene from the Book of Moses to others as a warning not to break the law. When our people were in the wilderness they murmured against GOD. The living GOD sent fiery serpents among the people, and they bit the people; and many died. Then those who remained alive confessed their sins and pleaded with Moses to intercede for them. The Lord instructed Moses to make a serpent of brass. Anyone who looked upon this serpent of brass suspended on the pole lived. By a look at the suspended serpent the poison would leave his system.

"And now this JESUS said that the Son of man must be suspended even as the serpent of brass and that whosoever believed in Him would not perish, but have eternal life. This was so contrary to all my beliefs concerning the Messiah that my mind was in a turmoil. Must the Messiah be suspended in the manner that criminals were crucified? How then could He be our King and lead us against the Romans? How could He establish the Kingdom? And must we as Israelites look upon this suspended Son of man? This JESUS must consider that we are just as great sinners as our forefathers in the wilderness. O yes, it was true of many like the Sadducees and Publicans. But surely that was not true of the Pharisees. Did this JESUS consider that I too was a sinner and had to look upon a suspended Messiah as my forefathers looked upon the serpent of brass? Is that the only way I could enter into the Kingdom of GOD?

"I left the presence of JESUS. No one had seen me. If my colleagues knew of my interview they did not indicate it to me. I congratulated myself that my interview was kept a secret. For several years I saw nothing of JESUS but I continued to hear about His miracles and teachings. My colleagues hated Him more and more, for some of the people believed that this JESUS was the Messiah. At one time they sent the guard to arrest Him. The guard was so impressed with His teachings that they did not dare to arrest Him. For this they were sternly rebuked. But I spoke up and said: '**Doth our law judge any man before it hear him and know what he doeth?**' They turned at me and said, '**Art thou also of Galilee? Search, and look; for out of Galilee ariseth no prophet**.' Cowardly I remained silent although I could have told them that Jonah and Nahum came forth from Galilee. I feared, however, to offend them and I thought it would be best to remain silent.

"They were determined to kill JESUS. I learned a few months later that they had contacted one of His disciples whom they bribed to betray Him. Then it happened. It seems that they seized JESUS in the Garden of Gethsemane. They hastily called the Sanhedrin together at midnight.

This was illegal. They did not call me for they suspected that I was sympathetic towards JESUS. In the morning Joseph of Arimathea told me what had happened. I was indignant when I heard that my colleagues had influenced Pilate to crucify JESUS. Joseph and I hastened to Golgotha the place where they crucified criminals.

"And there I beheld the terrible sight of JESUS crucified upon a cross. Tears filled my eyes for I was convinced that JESUS was a teacher sent from GOD. A teacher? Suddenly I remembered the words of JESUS: '**And as Moses lifted up the serpent into the wilderness, even so must the Son of man be lifted up; that whosoever believeth in Him should not perish, but have eternal life**.' JESUS was lifted up. JESUS is the Son of Man. JESUS is the Messiah. It was my Saviour and my GOD who hung on the cross. I believed. I believed.

"JESUS died on the cross. Joseph obtained permission to bury the body in the tomb. I brought about a hundred weight of myrrh and aloes and we anointed the body of the Lord. But the tomb could not contain my Lord. He arose on the third day and ascended into Heaven. Oh that you would behold the crucified Lord! He was lifted up even as Moses lifted the brazen serpent. Won't you behold Him! Look upon the crucified One with eyes of faith and you will not perish but possess life everlasting. May GOD cause you to be born a second time, 'for except a man be born again he cannot see the Kingdom of God.' "

day Andrew and I, along with James and John, left our nets and followed Him.

"I wish that I had time to tell you all that JESUS spoke and did. His teachings thrilled us. He gave sight to the blind, hearing to the deaf, and cleansed lepers. It mattered not to Him who a person was or how dreadful his disease. He helped him. He had love and compassion for all. Let me tell you of one incident.

"A certain ruler came and worshipped JESUS and said, '**My daughter is even now dead; but come and lay thy hand upon her, and she shall live**.' When we arrived at the house of Jairus we found the house full of people. They were weeping and wailing. The noise they made was terrific. JESUS said to the noisy crowd: '**Give place; for the maid is not dead but sleepeth**.' How they laughed Him to scorn and ridiculed Him. It made my blood boil. But JESUS took James, John and myself into the room where the young girl was. He put forth His hand and raised her. When the crowd saw the little girl alive they looked foolish, let me tell you. I was tempted to make fun of them, but I knew the Master would not approve.

"I was thrilled to be chosen along with eleven others to be apostles of our Lord. Among the other eleven were Andrew, James and John. Whereas before we were partners in the catching of fish now we were partners in catching men. Soon after, our Lord sent us on a preaching mission. We were to preach that the kingdom of Heaven was at hand. Also we were to heal the sick, cleanse the lepers, raise the dead, cast out devils. It was a wonderful experience to see the power of GOD working in the lives of others. We called upon all to repent of their sins.

"Sometime afterwards we were at Caesarea Philippi. There our Lord asked us: '**Whom do men say that I the Son of man am?**' We told Him that some said He was Elijah; others Jeremiah, or one of the prophets. He was disappointed with these answers. He turned to us and asked; '**But whom say ye that I am?**' For some time I had become convinced within my heart that JESUS was truly the Messiah and under the inspiration of the Spirit of GOD I was led to reply: '**Thou are the Christ, the Son of the Living God**.' JESUS graciously said to me: '**Blessed art thou, Simon Barjona: for flesh and blood hath not revealed it unto thee, but my Father which is in Heaven. And I say also unto thee, That thou are Peter, and upon this rock I will build my church and the gates of hell shall not prevail against it. And I will give unto thee the keys of Heaven: and whatsoever thou shalt bind on earth shall be bound in Heaven: and whatsoever thou shall loose on earth shall be loosed in Heaven.**'

"I must confess that I felt proud when our Lord said that. Evidently I was destined to take a big part in the Kingdom. But my Lord soon humbled me. JESUS began to tell what seemed very strange to us. He said that He must go to Jerusalem and suffer many things of the elders, the chief priests and scribes. He said that He would be killed and be raised again the third day. This annoyed and irritated me. How could they kill Him who was able to raise the dead? And if they killed Him how could He establish the Kingdom? The more I thought about this the more indignant I got. So I turned and rebuked the Lord for having such thoughts. But the Lord rebuked me and said: '**Get thee behind me, Satan: thou art an offense to me: for thou savourest not the things that be of God, but those that be of men.**'

"How that humbled me! Here I had exalted myself. Did not JESUS call me a stone and give me the keys of the Kingdom! But now He called me an offense and even Satan. I know now why He called me Satan. Satan wanted to tempt JESUS to establish a Kingdom without the cross. I spoke in ignorance and was justly rebuked and humbled.

"Six days later JESUS took James, John and myself up into a high mountain. While JESUS was praying we were startled to see Him transfigured before us. His face did shine as the sun, and His raiment was white as light. And behold we saw two men speaking with JESUS. They were Moses and Elijah. Strangely, they were speaking of the coming death of JESUS - of His crucifixion. We scarcely knew what to think or say and I blurted out: '**Lord, it is good for us to be here; if thou wilt, let us make here three tents; one for thee, one for Moses, and one for Elijah.**' I wanted to stay on the Mount forever. But while I was yet speaking, a bright

But just before His ascension He said: '**All power is given unto Me in Heaven and in earth. Go ye therefore and teach all nations, baptizing them in the name of the Father, and the Son and of the Holy Ghost. And Lo! I am with you alway even unto the end of the world. Amen**.' In obedience to His command I do testify to you that JESUS is the CHRIST, the son of the Living GOD. May you experience His pardoning grace even as I experienced it."

CHAPTER EIGHT "I Sold The Lord" by Judas Iscariot

"From the bottom-most pit of hell I lift up my voice in protest against my fate. I do not deserve the punishment which is meted out to me. One would think I were a fiend incarnate. All the dwellers in hell shrink from me as though I had committed the greatest crime in history. My crime was great. It was terrible. I did sell the Lord. But it was all due to a misunderstanding. It was due to a weak moment in my life. It was a sin any man could commit. Let me tell you my story.

"My name is Judas Iscariot. I was born in the Province of Judah in the country of Palestine. My father's name was Simon. He was well known throughout Judea as a man of deep religious convictions and an ardent patriot. It was his ambition to give me a thorough training in the law and prophets. The traditions of the elders also were carefully explained to me.

"The great interest of my father was the coming of the Messiah. It was his talk day and night. He told me that the Messiah would be like King David. As King David drove out the Philistines so would the Messiah drive out the Romans from our country. He pointed out the words of David in Psalm 72 concerning the Messiah: '**He shall have dominion also from sea to sea, and from the river unto the ends of the earth. Yea, all Kings shall fall down before Him: all nations shall serve Him**.'

"I remember asking father if that meant that our nation would be as powerful as the Romans who ruled over us. My father was angry at that question. He said that the Romans were not to be mentioned in the same breath as the nation of the Jews. The dominion of the Messiah, he said, would be greater and more extensive than that of the Romans. Our wealth would be a thousand times that of the Romans. And the Kingdom of the Messiah would rule over the rest of the world till the end of time.

"You can well imagine how that fired my imagination. I became as anxious for the coming of the Messiah as my father. Often I would wonder if the Messiah would come in my day. With my father I prayed earnestly that GOD would send the great Deliverer soon.

"GOD answered our prayers. I was nearing the age of thirty when I began to hear of a man by the name of JESUS. At the time I heard about Him He was teaching in Galilee. I heard that He taught in the synagogues and proclaimed the good news of the Kingdom. He had power to heal the sick. People told me that He healed every disease, even that of leprosy. Hundreds followed whithersoever he went.

"I determined to find Him and traveled to Galilee. I first saw Him as He was teaching a great multitude. There must have been at least two thousand people. His teaching was simple and with authority. I had never heard a scribe teach as He taught. He spoke of the Kingdom and the laws of the Kingdom. When He was through teaching they brought to Him the sick. I was amazed to behold Him casting out demons and restoring lunatics to their right mind. It mattered not what the disease was, He had power to heal.

"Upon observing Him it became my conviction that JESUS was the Messiah. He had the bearing of a king and He had the power of a king. Under His leadership surely Israel would be released from bondage to the Romans. I determined that I would become His disciple. It was not an easy decision to make. My business was prosperous. Yet if the Kingdom were to be established sacrifices would have to be made. And to sit at the feet of JESUS was the privilege of a lifetime. There was so much to learn about the Kingdom of GOD.

"It was a proud day for me to be chosen by JESUS to be one of the Twelve. We were especially chosen to be His witnesses and He took special pains to teach us the truths of the Kingdom. It was after He had chosen the Twelve that He delivered the sermon from the mount. It was thrilling to learn that we were to be the salt of the earth and the light of the world. JESUS told us, too, that we would even be blessed if we were persecuted for His sake. When JESUS finished His teachings 'the **people were astonished at His**

doctrine: for He taught them as one having authority, and not as the scribes.'

"Another proud day for the Twelve was when we were sent out on a mission. We went forth preaching the good news of the Kingdom. We urged people to repent because the Kingdom of GOD was at hand. The Master gave us power to heal. Just by a touch of the hand I gave sight to the blind and hearing to the deaf. Even the lepers were cleansed. By my command demons were cast out. It was not difficult to visualize the establishment of the Kingdom throughout the world.

"Because the Master recognized my business ability He appointed me to have charge of the treasury bag. We received donations from people who felt grateful for what the Master did for them. JESUS could have received much more but He did not seem to be interested in becoming rich. And what He did receive He wanted to give away immediately. Sometimes there was hardly any left to buy food for us. I questioned the wisdom of giving so much for the poor. The Master was over-generous. That seemed to be about His only fault.

"We were on the whole a very harmonious group. There was only once that we had a serious quarrel. John and James stole a march on us. Through their mother they asked the Master to give them the most prominent places in the kingdom. The two brothers wanted to sit on each side of the throne of JESUS. We were angry when we heard about it. After all I was just as qualified and perhaps even more so than James and John to have the prominent place in the Kingdom. It would require a man who could handle money. Peter and Matthew thought they were the best qualified. As a matter of fact all twelve of us quarreled about it. But the Master soon settled the argument.

"Jesus said to us: '**Ye know that the princes of the Gentiles exercise dominion over them, and they that are great exercise authority upon them. But it shall not be so among you; but whosoever will be great among you, let him be your minister; and whosoever will be chief among you, let him be your servant**.' This statement bothered me. I thought surely in the

Kingdom we as apostles would lord it over others - that we would live as Roman princes. But now the Master spoke of us as being the servants of others.

"Then another thing began to bother me. JESUS was not winning many of the prominent men of Israel to His cause. The scribes and Pharisees opposed Him. It was not hard to see that they hated JESUS. This seemed to me detrimental to the cause. They were men of influence and power in our nation. People respected their opinion. Many feared to join themselves to JESUS because it would subject them to criticism of these leaders of Israel. All this hindered the establishment of the kingdom.

"Other people left JESUS because of His teachings. After He fed five thousand people by a miracle, it was the desire of the multitude to make Him a king. JESUS would have none of it. He also rebuked the people by stating they were following Him only because of the miracle of the loaves and fishes. Then JESUS said: '**I am the living bread which came down from Heaven; if any man eat of this bread, he shall live forever; and the bread that I will give is my flesh, which I will give for the life of the world**.' When they asked how He could give His flesh to eat, JESUS stated: '**Whoso eateth my flesh and drinketh my blood, hath eternal life**.' When some of the disciples heard that they left Him. One could scarcely blame them when He talked about eating his flesh and drinking His blood. As I was thinking along this manner, JESUS suddenly said: '**Have not I chosen you twelve, and one of you is a devil?**' I was startled because it seemed as though He read my mind. But surely He would not call me a devil just because I was thinking that He was not handling the situation right?'

"It must have become apparent to JESUS that He could not overcome the opposition of the scribes and Pharisees. He began to speak about them seeking to kill Him. He spoke about being crucified. That, of course, would be the end of the Kingdom. If crucified how could He lead us to be a mighty Kingdom? What profit would there be in following Him? It was a lost cause. I had wasted my time and opportunities. How had I ever been so foolish as to follow one who would be crucified as a criminal?

"As these questions entered into my mind, I began to think as to how I could obtain profit out of this situation. My eyes fell on the treasury bag. Ah! Why not keep part of this money? Surely part was mine. I had followed JESUS for several years without wages. I had given up my business and received nothing in return. It was only fair that I should keep part. So I began withdrawing small amounts. I wondered whether JESUS knew. Sometimes it seemed as if He looked right into my heart. I began to resent Him. When He preached about theft it seemed as though He looked at me with a warning. But why should He think it was theft when it was really mine?

"I began to look for large donations. The more that was given the more I could take. Six days before the Passover we were entertained in the home of Martha and Mary. Mary took a pound of ointment of spikenard and anointed the feet of JESUS. What a waste this was for the spikenard was very costly. I cried out: '**Why was not this ointment sold for three hundred pence, and given to the poor?**' It would mean about a hundred pence for me. But JESUS talked about this being an anointing for His burial. Three hundred pence wasted in a moment.

"This was the climax as far as I was concerned. I knew that the elders and chief priest wanted to kill JESUS but they were afraid of the reaction of the people. They wanted to take Him when He was away from the multitude. So a few days before the Passover I went to the chief priests. They were amazed to see me but when I told them what I wanted to do they could hardly contain themselves for joy. I asked them how much they would give me if I would deliver Him into their hands. We bargained for some time. All that I could get out of them was thirty pieces of silver, the price of a slave. However, it was better than nothing and it would require very little effort. From that time I sought an opportunity to deliver Him according to our bargain.

"At night we began the Passover Supper. While we were eating, JESUS suddenly said: '**Verily I say unto you, that one of you shall betray me.**' Fear struck my heart for I thought that JESUS would uncover me before the others. However, they all began to ask Him, '**Lord, is it I?**' Not one suspected me. JESUS tried to scare me by saying: 'Woe unto that man through whom the Son of man is betrayed! good were it for that man if he had not been born.' So I said aside to JESUS with a sneer, 'Is it I, Rabbi?' He said, 'Thou hast said.' Shortly afterwards He said, 'That thou doest, do quickly.'

"I went according to plan to the chief priest. I knew that JESUS intended to go into the garden of Gethsemane to pray. He would perhaps take James, John and Peter with Him. That would be a fine opportunity to seize him. The chief priest and elders had gathered quite a sizable mob who were armed with staves and swords. I told them that I would kiss the one whom they should seize. When I saw JESUS in the garden I went up to Him and said, 'Hail, Rabbi,' and kissed Him. Then the mob laid hands on Him and took Jesus and led Him to the chief priests.

"I did not go along with the mob but went to my lodging. There I counted the thirty pieces of silver again and again. In my mind I tried to figure how this money could start me in business. I had to make up for the three years wasted. I could hardly sleep in anticipation of how rich I would become.

"In the morning I went to the place where the council was held. There was great excitement. They had tried JESUS during the night and condemned Him to death. Now they determined that they would deliver Him to Pilate the governor so that He could be crucified. They bound Him and led Him away.

"As they led Him away bound, suddenly I realized that He was going to His death. They had condemned Him to death. But He was innocent of any crime. He had done no wrong. He had done nothing worthy of death. Yet they were going to have Him crucified as a criminal. And I - I was responsible. I betrayed an innocent man. I had sold the Lord. I had sold the Lord.

"Perhaps there was still time to save Him. I ran to the chief priest and elders and cried out: 'I have sinned in that I betrayed innocent blood.' But all they said was: 'What is that to us? see thou to it.' I flung the thirty pieces of silver down in front of them and ran out.

"I did not mean that they should crucify the Lord. Yet I had sold Him. I sold Him for the price of a slave - thirty pieces of silver. Would that I could undo what I had done! I betrayed innocent blood. I betrayed innocent blood. How could I face the future with the knowledge that I had betrayed One who was righteous and innocent? And all for thirty pieces of silver. I could not face the future. There was only one thing left for me to do and that was to end it all. I would enter into the darkness of oblivion. Only by so doing I would escape my burning conscience. By hanging myself I would escape the torment of my mind. And so I hung myself.

"I awakened in hell. Escape? Escape? My conscience burns with a thousand-fold heat. All that goes through my mind is that I sold the Lord. I sold the Lord. I seem to hold in my hands thirty pieces of silver. They burn like hot lead in my hands. For the price of a slave I betrayed innocent blood - the blood of the Son of GOD. And all because I misunderstood the nature of the Kingdom. All because of my love of money. Surely it was a sin that anyone could commit. Why, O why, must I be punished so severely?"

CHAPTER NINE "I Condemned JESUS To Be Crucified" by Pilate

"My name is Pontius Pilate. For centuries I have washed my hands in protest against being condemned to hell. My greatest sin has been declared to be the unjust condemnation of CHRIST. But I did not realize that JESUS was the Son of the living GOD. I worked hard to free him. Seven times I declared that he was innocent of any crime. I was forced by the people to condemn him to crucifixion. Openly before the nation of the Jews I took water and washed my hands, protesting by this action that I was innocent of the blood of him whom I felt at the time was a righteous man. And I continue the washing of my hands to this day in protest of my being adjudged guilty of unrighteous judgment. It was neither my will nor desire to condemn JESUS. It was due to political expediency. But in spite of my protest the stain of guilt is still upon my hands. I have discovered nothing in hell which will wipe off the stains of sin.

"However, let me tell you my story of that eventful day when I officially condemned JESUS to be crucified. It was while I was procurator over Judea by appointment of Emperor Tiberius. You will see how I was forced into that action against my will and that I am actually innocent of the blood of JESUS CHRIST.

"It was before seven o'clock on a Friday morning that I was summoned by the Jews to pass judgment on a certain JESUS whom they had arrested and tried before the Sanhedrin, the Jewish court. With my wife I was in residence at the Palace in Jerusalem. It was our custom to stay in Jerusalem during the Jewish Passover Feast. Ordinarily I would have tried this man within the Palace but the Jews had a prejudice against entering into it. They claimed that it would defile them and would prevent them from taking part in their Feast. I yielded to their prejudice and superstition and met with them outside of the Palace.

"I immediately asked them what their accusation was against this JESUS. Evidently they expected me to condemn the man without any formal accusation and without a trial. But I refused to sit down to judgment without a formal accusation. They tried to get around my request by stating: '**If this man were not an evildoer, we should not have delivered him up unto thee.**'

What kind of a judge did they think I was by insinuating that I should condemn a man simply on their statement that he was an evildoer! Knowing that their action was based on a question of their religious law I replied: '**Take him yourselves, and judge him according to your law.**'

"I thought that they would take advantage of this offer but their reply was: '**It is not lawful for us to put any man to death**.' So - they wanted this man to be crucified. Our Roman government had taken away from the Jewish Court the right to pass the death sentence. What amazed me was that they wanted the death sentence passed upon this man because they said he was perverting their nation by forbidding to give taxes to Caesar and because he claimed to be a king. They did not fool me by this accusation. They had no love for Caesar nor were they zealous in paying taxes. The hypocrites! However, I did think it wise to question this JESUS about his claim to be a king. If he was thinking of leading a rebellion against Rome, I would condemn him immediately.

"I went into the palace where my soldiers had taken him. I summoned him to me and asked: '**Art thou the King of the Jews?**' He had the impertinence to reply: '**Sayest thou this of thyself, or did others tell it thee concerning me?**' I answered: '**Am I a Jew? Thine own nation and the chief priests delivered thee unto me: what hast thou done?**'

"Then this JESUS gave a strange answer. It was fantastic. He said: '**My kingdom is not of this world; if my kingdom were of this world, then would my servants fight, that I should not be delivered to the Jews: but now is my kingdom not from hence.**' How could he have a kingdom if it was not of this world? How could he establish a kingdom without fighting? The man was out of his mind. However, it was evident that he did not plan to set up a rival kingdom to Rome. It was not his plan to lead a rebellion against

Caesar. That was my only concern. And yet he seemed to think that he was some kind of king. So I asked him: '**Art thou a king then?**' He answered in the affirmative. He said: '**Thou sayest that I am a king. To this end have I been born, and to this end am I come into the world, that I should bear witness unto the truth. Everyone that is of the truth heareth my voice.**'

"Truth! Everyone that is of the truth would hear his voice! I supposed he thought that if I knew the truth that I would be his follower - his subject. How ridiculous! Who in the Empire of Rome knew the truth? The Stoics? The Epicureans? These fanatic Jews? This JESUS? Truth does not exist. You cannot believe any man. So I replied: '**What is truth?**' Nevertheless, I determined to release this man. The kingdom he had in mind was one of fantasy and not like the kingdom of Rome. He was not out to rebel against Caesar. The idea of putting this man to death for his fantastic ideas was abhorrent.

"So I went outside of the Palace and spoke to the Jews. I told them frankly that I could find no crime in this JESUS. But the chief priests made one accusation after another. Not one amounted to anything. They also stated that he had stirred up the people in the province of Galilee. Herod Antipas was Tetrarch over Galilee. He and I were enemies because I had put some Galileans to death without consulting him. And so I thought here was my chance to make up with him and to get out of my difficulty concerning this JESUS whom I felt to be innocent. Therefore I sent him to Herod.

"The chief priests also had gone to Herod. From what I heard later they vehemently accused JESUS of many things. But JESUS refused to answer their accusations and would make no reply to Herod. Herod and his soldiers set JESUS at nought. They mocked his pretensions to kingship. They arrayed him in gorgeous apparel and sent him back to me. Herod felt that JESUS should come under my jurisdiction. That was a nice gesture on his part and we became friends from that day.

"So I again called together the chief priests, the rulers, and the people, and said to them: '**Ye brought unto me this man, as one that perverteth the people: and behold, I, having examined** him before you, found no fault in this man touching those things whereof ye accuse him: no, nor yet Herod: for he sent him back unto us; and behold, nothing worthy of death hath been done by him. I will therefore chastise him, and release him.'

"It was my thought that by scourging him it would give sufficient satisfaction to his persecutors. Then another thought struck me. It was my custom to release any prisoner at the request of the Jews during the Passover Feast. I had a notable prisoner by the name of Barabbas. He was guilty of insurrection, murder, and theft. He was not particularly loved of the people. Surely if it came to a choice between Barabbas and JESUS the people would choose JESUS. After all, it was only because the Jewish leaders were jealous of JESUS that they wanted his death. By giving this choice of Barabbas or JESUS I would put a wedge between the people and the leaders. When I asked whether it would be Barabbas or JESUS they were not ready for their decision. I gave them a little time to think it over.

"While I was waiting for their answer my wife sent me a message. It read: '**Have thou nothing to do with that righteous man: for I have suffered many things this day in a dream because of him**.' This message startled me and - I must confess - frightened me. Who is this JESUS? Are the gods interested in him that they would send a message to my wife in a dream? What manner of person is he?

"As I reflected on this dream of my wife the multitude gave a sign that they were ready with an answer. I asked them whether it was JESUS whom they wanted released. They cried out: '**Away with this man, and release unto us Barabbas**.' This stunned me for I felt sure they would ask for a righteous man rather than a thief and murderer. I learned later that the chief priests had influenced the people to that decision. I cried out to them: '**What then shall I do unto Jesus which is called Christ?**' And they replied: '**Crucify him, crucify him**.' I cried out: '**Why, what evil hath this man done? I have found no cause of death in him**.' Then the frenzied mob cried out the more: '**Crucify him, crucify him, crucify him!**'

61

"I knew that nothing would still them but the crucifixion of JESUS. With reluctance I gave way to their will. I did not want trouble. However, to show them that it was their decision and not mine, I called for a basin of water. I washed my hands before that entire multitude and declared:

'**I am innocent of the blood of this righteous man: see ye to it!**' They accepted the responsibility by crying out: '**His blood be on us, and on our children**.' Then I released Barabbas and ordered JESUS to be scourged.

"The soldiers did a thorough job in this scourging. The strongest of them ripped open the back of JESUS with a cruel scourge. The men thought they would also have some fun with him. They heard that he had claimed to be a king. So in mockery they crowned him. They plaited a crown out of thorns and pressed it into his brow. They put a purple robe on him and placed a reed in his hand as a scepter. Each one bowed before him and cried: '**Hail, king of the Jews!**' Then each soldier spit upon him. After this treatment they brought him to me. I am not easily moved. But knowing that he was innocent, it did move me to see him, scourged and crowned with thorns. The thought struck me that if the people saw him now they would be satisfied and no longer demand his crucifixion. It would be worth trying for I was troubled about this man.

"I went out to the people again and said to them: '**Behold, I bring him out to you, that ye may know that I find no crime in him**.' Then my soldiers led JESUS out, wearing the crown of thorns and the purple garment. What a pitiful object he presented to the people: pale as death; his face covered with blood and spittle; his brow pierced with sharp thorns; and his hair matted with blood. But the sight of him did not change their hearts and again I heard that cry: '**Crucify him, crucify him, crucify him!**' I did not want that responsibility and said to them: '**Take him yourselves, and crucify him: for I find no fault in him**.'

"The Jews then made a statement which sent fear into my heart. They said: '**We have a law, and by that law he ought to die, because he made himself the Son of God**.' The Son of GOD? The Son of GOD? What manner of man is this JESUS? He impressed me as a righteous man but was he actually a son of one of the gods? I was not religious but I knew that sometimes the gods did visit the earth. Into what trouble was I getting? I better question this JESUS again. I ordered the soldiers to take him into the Palace.

"I asked him to tell me who he really was. He gave no answer. This angered me and I said: '**Speakest thou not unto me? knowest thou not that I have power to release thee, and have power to crucify thee?**' To this he gave reply: '**Thou wouldest have no power against me, except it were given thee from above: therefore he that delivered me unto thee hath greater sin.**' This frightened me all the more because I did not desire to have the vengeance of the gods upon me. Therefore I worked hard to influence the Jews to be satisfied with the scourging I had given him and consent to his release.

"But the Jews cried out: '**If thou release this man, thou art not Caesar's friend: everyone that maketh himself a king speaketh against Caesar.**' So they would accuse me of treason. This was a ridiculous charge. And yet I would not desire to have the Emperor hear even a false charge of treason. My enemies at Rome might try to make capital of it. There were many that wanted my position. Why should I risk my position and reputation for this JESUS? I knew that he was innocent and time and time again I declared that he was innocent of any crime. I labored hard to influence the Jews to be satisfied with his release. But I could not go against their will. That would not be good politics. They might petition the Emperor to remove me. Again I called the soldiers to bring out JESUS. I placed him in the charge of the centurion and ordered him to proceed with the crucifixion. They led him away to Calvary where criminals were crucified.

"From that time on one ill fortune after another was my lot. A Samaritan impostor promised his countrymen that he would show them where Moses had hidden certain golden vessels of the tabernacle. He gathered a multitude. I learned that they carried arms. I ordered my soldiers to attack them. Many of the Samaritans were slain. A complaint was made to Vitellius, my immediate superior. He appointed a new procurator and ordered me to proceed to Rome to give an account of what happened to the Emperor. Here again ill fortune followed me. Emperor Tiberius died before I arrived in Rome. I tried my best to influence Emperor Caligula to appoint me to office. But he was influenced against me by my enemies and I was banished to Gaul.

'"My life in Gaul was unbearable. My wife did not help matters. She constantly reminded me that I had failed to heed the warning of her dream about that righteous man JESUS who was crucified in Judea. Finally I could not bear the torment of my life upon earth. I determined to commit suicide. Why bear torment on earth when death will remove it? Torment on earth? It is Heaven in comparison with the eternal torment of hell. The guilt of a thousand sins sears my hands with red hot flames. Nothing will wash away that searing guilt! I wash and wash to no avail. And the deepest stain of guilt - that which sears with greatest intensity - is the condemnation of the righteous man JESUS whom I know now to be the Son of GOD, the Judge of the earth."

CHAPTER TEN "I Was Saved At The Eleventh Hour" by the Dying Thief

"I was saved at the eleventh hour. It is scarcely believable that GOD would save such a wretch as I was. Surely our GOD is gracious and powerful to save. I know that GOD saved me so that all might have hope. If GOD saved such a sinner as I, He can save anyone. But let me tell you my story.

"I was born in the city of Jerusalem in the land of Canaan. My parents were very poor. They had no interest in giving me an education. Of course, like all Jews I was exposed to religion. While my family did not attend the services of the synagogue very regularly they did partake in the religious feasts. Particularly they kept the Feast of the Passover. They felt that by so doing they fulfilled all the requirements of religion.

"Jerusalem was a city of great wickedness. Vice touched young and old. As a youngster I joined a gang that went about doing mischief of all kinds. Because I got into many scrapes with the authorities my parents drove me from home. This satisfied me because I could not tolerate restrictions of any kind.

"When I became older I joined a gang of thieves headed by Barabbas, a notorious robber of the day. He was hated by all the people and greatly feared. He would stop at nothing. He took part in a number of insurrections and did not stop at murder. It was our special delight to plunder the pilgrims who visited Jerusalem during the feast days. Generally they were rich and had much money on their persons. The Passover Feast brought many of them from all parts of the world to Jerusalem.

"Our great fear were the Romans who ruled our nation. We did not fear the local guard. We despised them. But the Romans would not stand for any nonsense. Anyone caught stealing was given the death sentence. He would be crucified on a cross. We took care that we would not fall into their hands. However, just previous to the Passover we grew too careless and were drinking too much. We had just made a rich haul when the Roman guard came upon us. Three of us were caught including our leader, Barabbas. We were brought before Pilate. There wasn't much we could say for we were caught with the stolen goods. Pilate sentenced us to be crucified. And he ordered the Roman guard to scourge us first.

"Scourging is a cruel torture. We were stripped and bound to a pillar. Then one of the soldiers took a scourge of leather tongs to beat us. At the end of each tong was a piece of iron. This he lashed against our backs. The other two were scourged first and it made me sick to look at them. The instrument of torture tore out pieces of flesh and the veins were exposed. Then one of them started on me. How I cursed him for the suffering he caused. That made them all laugh and he increased the force of his blows. My whole back was a mass of raw and bleeding flesh. When they finished they flung us back into the dungeon and told us that the crucifixion would be the next day.

"Things looked very dark. It seemed as though all was lost and that we would suffer the torture of the crucifixion on the morrow. But while there is life there is hope. In spite of our weak condition we spoke of the possibility of escape. It seemed, however, hopeless. Then suddenly I thought of the custom of Pilate of releasing a criminal during the Passover. I told my friends about it. I told them how Pilate would give our countrymen the choice of the deliverance of some prisoner. We could hardly conceive of any of them asking for our release for we were hated by all. I even doubted whether my parents would ask for my release. Yet I felt that I had a better chance than Barabbas for the people hated him more than us all. Barabbas himself felt that his chance of deliverance was very slim.

"Early next morning there was a stir of excitement among the Roman guards. We heard them talking about the capture of a certain JESUS who claimed to be a king. It seemed to me that I had heard about him. There were rumors that he was a miracle worker and that he claimed to be the Messiah. I never paid much attention to such things for I felt that religion was a racket. I felt that the priests and the Pharisees were religious hypocrites. We wondered among ourselves what sentence this JESUS would receive.

"Suddenly the door of our dungeon was opened and one of the guards spoke to Barabbas and said that the Jews had asked for his release. Barabbas would not believe him for he could not conceive how anyone would ask for his release. But the guard insisted that it was true. He said that the people had been given a choice between JESUS and Barabbas and that they had chosen him. Pilate had given the order for his release. Barabbas was almost dazed with joy and walked out a free man.

"My friend and I looked at each other with amazement. Then we cursed our countrymen for not choosing one of us. Why did they not choose one of us rather than Barabbas whom they hated so violently? Nevertheless his release gave us hope. Perhaps some miracle would happen to us. But, alas, we seemed doomed. The guards came and told us to get ready to be taken to Calvary. They said as soon as they were finished scourging this JESUS they would start. I heard some of them planning to have fun with this JESUS because he claimed to be the king of the Jews. They said that they would make him a king by giving him a crown of thorns and a scarlet robe. They took him into the common hall and summoned the whole band of soldiers.

"After they had finished torturing him they came for us. They made us bear the crosses on which we were to be hung. With curiosity I looked at this JESUS who was also compelled to bear a cross. His face was covered with blood from the thorns that had been pressed into his brow. I could well imagine that his back was covered with stripes from the scourging. He seemed weak and hardly able to bear his cross. As a matter of fact they compelled a country fellow to bear his cross for him.

"This JESUS seemed to be a man of importance for a great multitude turned out to see him and a number of women bewailed and lamented him. JESUS told them not to weep for him but to weep for themselves. No one wept for me. Not even my parents came out. Both my friend and I cursed the crowd and the soldiers.

"We arrived at the hated place of Calvary. They gave us a drink of wine mixed with myrrh. This was to deaden the pain. I drunk the stuff greedily. I noticed that JESUS refused to drink his. The fool,

67

I thought. They began to nail my hands and feet to the cross. How I struggled. It took three of the strongest soldiers to hold me while a fourth did the nailing. They tore my flesh with the nails. This JESUS did not struggle. He prayed. He seemed like a lamb led to the slaughter. While they were nailing him I heard him pray: '**Father, forgive them; for they know not what they do**.' I despised him for this prayer. The Roman brutes knew what they were doing. How could he pray for them after they had tortured us! I could not curse them enough.

"In spite of the wine and myrrh I suffered terribly. My bones seemed to separate one from the other and the pain from the nails was indescribable. I was placed on the right of JESUS and my friend on the left. They had made a sign and placed it on the center cross. It read: '**This is, JESUS the king of the Jews**.' Evidently this JESUS: thought that he was the King prophesied in our Scriptures. He thought that he was the Messiah. A cross was a very poor substitute for the throne of David.

"JESUS remained the center of attraction. The crowd paid no attention to us. The people that passed by stuck out their tongues at him and mocked him. The chief priests along with the scribes and elders cried out to him: '**If thou art the Son of God, come down from the cross**.' Then they laughed at him. They cried out: '**He saved others; himself he cannot save. He is the King of Israel; let him now come down from the cross, and' we will believe on him. He trusteth on God; let him deliver him now, if he desireth him: for he said, I am the Son of God.**'

"I must confess that we joined in the mockery. We railed at him and challenged him to perform a miracle and release us from our crosses. Surely the Messiah would be able to do this. Surely the Messiah would not die the shameful death of a crucified criminal. But though we reproached him he did not reproach us. Although he was reviled by the religious leaders he did not revile them. This amazed me.

"What if this JESUS were the Messiah? He did not seem like an ordinary man. What if he were the King whom GOD said would deliver us? Perhaps this man will rise from the dead and establish

68

the promised kingdom. I can scarcely explain how I began to think differently about JESUS. I know now that it was the Spirit of GOD who convicted me. JESUS seemed so noble and righteous. I felt so vile. My soul was black with sin but JESUS had committed no crime worthy of death.

"My friend continued his railing at JESUS. He cried out: '**Art not thou the Messiah? save thyself and us**.' But I rebuked my friend and said: '**Dost thou not even fear God, seeing thou art in the same condemnation? and we indeed justly; for we receive the due reward of our deeds: but this man hath done nothing amiss**.' Ah yes, I realized suddenly that I was not only under the condemnation of man but also under the condemnation of GOD. Fear filled my heart at the thought of the judgment of GOD.

"I came under the firm conviction that JESUS was the Messiah. I believed that He was truly the Son of GOD - the promised King. Surely He could save me. I cried out to Him: '**Jesus, remember me when thou comest in thy kingdom**.' Yes, if He would only remember me when He entered into His glory. But how could I expect that? I had railed at Him. I was vile. I was a thief. I was a blasphemer. I was guilty of a thousand sins. How could I expect the Messiah to remember me? Yet had He not prayed for the forgiveness of the Roman brutes? Would He not do the same for me?

"Then I heard Him speaking these wonderful words: '**Verily I say unto thee, To-day shalt thou be with me in Paradise**.' I was more than to be remembered. I was to be with the Messiah in Paradise. Paradise! I was suffering the pains of hell and death. The scourging, the nails, the racking pain of body was but a foretaste of hell. And even more painful was the realization that my soul was vile and that I was condemned before the Holy GOD. And now Paradise. The Son of GOD assured me that even today I was to be with Him in Paradise!

"Somehow I forgot the nails, the cross, and the tormenting crowd. Peace Hooded my soul. JESUS the Messiah, the Son of GOD, the King of Israel had given me the promise of Paradise. It seemed even at the moment that I had been translated into Paradise. I was no longer under condemnation. The gates of Heaven beckoned me. Yes, I still suffered; but in a few hours I would be in the presence of GOD with my Saviour. My sins were forgiven. In a few hours indeed I entered into Heaven. It is Paradise.

"And now as my voice reaches across the generations I would testify of the love of GOD and the compassion of the Saviour. JESUS is the Son of GOD. JESUS is the Messiah. JESUS is the King of kings. Oh, that all would turn to Him. I was saved at the eleventh hour. My friend on the other cross died under condemnation. Hearken to the voice of JESUS now. Cry out to Him for salvation. Then you, too, will hear the most wonderful words ever spoken: '**Verily I say unto thee, To-day shalt thou be with me in Paradise**.'

CHAPTER ELEVEN "I Walked With The Risen Lord" by Cleopas

"My name is Cleopas. During my life upon earth I became a disciple of an extraordinary person whose name was JESUS. I first heard of him through one who was both my physician and friend. Luke was his name. He told me of some of the teachings of JESUS and of the miracles which he performed. I heard JESUS teach and with my own eyes I beheld him perform miracles. I became convinced that he was a prophet of the living GOD of Israel. At every opportunity I heard him teach about the living GOD.

"It was my constant amazement that the religious leaders of my nation did not recognize in JESUS a prophet of GOD. Surely he gave every evidence that GOD was with him. But the Pharisees, the scribes, and the chief priests hated him. We felt confident, however, that JESUS would overcome their opposition and that He would free our nation and establish the Kingdom of GOD. We felt that JESUS would redeem Israel.

"Little did I realize the intensity of their hatred. Finally they succeeded in bribing one of his own apostles. The Sanhedrin was called at night and the Court judged JESUS guilty of blasphemy. They took him to Pilate. He did not want to condemn JESUS to death. Such was the hatred of the religious rulers that they threatened to place a charge of treason against Pilate. So he yielded to their influence and ordered JESUS to be crucified.

"I was in Jerusalem at the time. I had traveled from my home in the village of Emmaus to Jerusalem in order to partake of the Passover Feast and also to be near JESUS. It was rumored that he was to be in Jerusalem. It was my hope that the leaders in Israel would recognize JESUS as a prophet of GOD. It was on the Sabbath that I learned that JESUS had been crucified on the day before. This news stunned me. I felt that all was lost.

"It so happened that I met Luke who was equally stunned with the terrible news that JESUS had been crucified. I asked him to travel with me to Emmaus on the morrow which was the first day of the week. He agreed. He did not know what to do with himself since JESUS was now dead. We could not leave early that next day as Luke had some business to perform and he wanted to see Peter. So we left about noon.

"Luke was a man who could gather news. As we walked to Emmaus he told me more of the things that had occurred. He obtained some of his information from Peter. First he told me about Judas. He had sold the Master for thirty pieces of silver and betrayed him in the garden of Gethsemane with a kiss. Later he was filled with remorse and hung himself. I told Luke that is exactly what he should have done. How he must have pained JESUS with that kiss of betrayal.

"Then Luke told me that JESUS was further pained by the denial of Peter. Peter had boasted that he would never forsake the Master. But he denied him three times and also with curses. Peter, however, was brokenhearted about his denial and actually wept. He wished that it were possible to confess his repentance to JESUS. But, alas, JESUS is dead.

"I asked Luke to tell me what happened at Pilate's court. He told me that the people under the influence of the chief priests had called for his crucifixion. Pilate ordered him to be scourged. The Roman soldiers mocked him by pressing a crown of thorns into his head and pretending that he was king of our nation. I was amazed when Luke told me that JESUS prayed for the forgiveness of these Roman brutes as they were nailing him to the cross. I would have cursed them to their faces. But that is just like the Master. How often he prayed for those who despitefully used him. Luke was so filled with emotion that he could hardly tell me of the sufferings which JESUS bore on the cross.

"We were puzzled about a report we heard from Mary Magdalene and the other women. They went early to the tomb in which JESUS was laid. They found the tomb empty and beheld a vision of angels. I heard that John and Peter had investigated this story and found the tomb empty. We thought that someone had taken his body to another place. Whether it was a friend or an enemy we did not know.

"While we were discussing this mysterious event, a stranger joined us and asked: '**What manner of communications are these that ye have one to another, as ye walk, and are sad?**' I answered: '**Art thou only a stranger in Jerusalem, and hast not known the things which are come to pass there in these days?**' Evidently he did not know for he asked: '**What things?**'

"I replied to him in this way: '**Why, concerning Jesus of Nazareth, who was a prophet mighty in deed and word before God and all the people. But the chief priests and our rulers delivered him to be condemned to death, and have crucified him. And we trusted that it had been he which should have redeemed Israel: and beside all this, today is the third day since these things were done. Yea and certain women also of our company made us astonished, who were early at the sepulchre; and when they found not his body they came, saying, that they had also seen a vision of angels, which said that he was alive. And certain of them which were with us went to the sepulchre, and found it even so as the women had said: but him they saw not.**'

"The man gave a rather rebuking reply to this information which I gave him. He said: '**O fools, and slow of heart to believe all that the prophets have spoken: ought not Christ to have suffered these things, and to enter into his glory?**' Luke asked him what he meant.

"The stranger replied: 'I mean that Moses and the Prophets spoke of the sufferings of CHRIST. Does it not state in the first book of Moses: I will put enmity between thee and the woman, and between thy seed and her seed; it shall bruise thy head, and thou shalt bruise his heel. The CHRIST is the seed of the woman. Before the seed of the woman could bruise the head of Satan, Satan would bruise his heel. CHRIST was to be bruised. And is it not true that Satan and his demons were present with all their cruelty at the crucifixion? Was not JESUS bruised?'

"Yes, JESUS was bruised. Luke and I acknowledged that Satan was in the hearts of Judas, the chief priests, Pilate, and the soldiers. Only under the influence of Satan could they be so cruel to him who did nothing but good. But did the Scriptures reveal that the

Messiah would have to suffer in this cruel fashion? I asked him that.

"The stranger replied: 'The Scriptures do clearly reveal it. How were the Israelites delivered from the bondage of Egypt? Was it not by the blood of the Lamb spread upon the lintels and the door posts? Blood had to be shed before deliverance came to the children of Israel. And do not the Tabernacle and the Temple declare that truth? How is atonement made for the sinning Israelites? Is it not through blood? The High Priest cannot approach the Holy of Holies except through the shedding and sprinkling of the blood. Lambs are sacrificed daily for sin in the Temple. And then was it not John the Baptist who cried out at the sight of JESUS: Behold the Lamb of GOD who taketh away the sin of the world. Since JESUS was the Lamb of GOD how could he save the world except through the shedding of his blood?'

"He was exactly right about what John the Baptist had said about JESUS. It was Andrew, Peter's brother, who had told us about it. But this suffering on the part of the Messiah still puzzled Luke and me. Luke asked him how could it be that the Messiah would be betrayed by one of his own disciples and denied by another.

"In answer the man quoted from the Scriptures. He said: 'The Psalmist has declared: **Yea, mine own familiar friend, in whom I trusted, which did eat of my bread, hath lifted up his heel against me**. That explains Judas. And Zechariah the prophet has stated: **I will smite the shepherd, and the sheep of the flock shall be scattered abroad**. That explains Peter - and also the other disciples.

"This convicted Luke because he was present at Pilate's judgment hall when the people cried out for the crucifixion of JESUS. He, too, was afraid to call out for his deliverance. This he confessed to the stranger and said: 'Oh, sir, I also deserted JESUS. But do the Scriptures say that the Messiah was to be spit upon and crucified like a common criminal?'

"Again the stranger quoted from the Scriptures. He replied: 'The prophet Isaiah said concerning the Messiah: I gave my back to the smiters, and my cheeks to them that plucked off the hair: I hid not my face from shame and spitting. Isaiah also stated that the Messiah was to be numbered with the transgressors. But if you really want to listen to the heart beats of the Messiah as they are prophesied in the Scriptures hear these words of the Psalmist David: **My God, my God, why hast thou forsaken me? Why art thou so far from helping me, and from the words of my groanings? Our fathers trusted in thee: they trusted, and thou didst deliver them. But I am a worm, and no man; a reproach of men, and despised of the people. All they that see me laugh me to scorn; they shoot out the lip, they shake the head, saying, He trusted on the Lord that he would deliver him: let him deliver him, seeing he delighted in him. I am poured out like water, and all my bones are out of joint: my heart is like wax; it is melted within me. My strength is dried up like a potsherd; and my tongue cleaveth to my jaws; and thou hast brought me into the dust of death. For dogs have compassed me: the assembly of the wicked have inclosed me: they pierced my hands and my feet. I may count all my bones. They look and stare upon me. They part my garments among them, and cast lots upon my vesture**. These are the words of the Psalmist David and they are prophetic of the sufferings of the Messiah.'

"As the stranger quoted these words my heart was stirred. Because I loved the Master I had attempted to keep out of my mind the sufferings which he endured on that terrible cross at Golgotha. But these words of David made me realize the awful anguish of the cross. There was the scorn of the people who surrounded the cross like a pack of yelping dogs. How that must have pained JESUS. How horrible was the piercing of his hands and feet; the dryness of death; the disjointing of his bones; and being forsaken by GOD whom he loved so dearly. Luke pointed out to me that the soldiers had gambled for the garment of JESUS even as the Psalmist had prophesied. But I still could not help thinking why it would be necessary for the Messiah to suffer in this terrible way. So I asked this man who had joined us as to the necessity of the Messiah's death.

"He answered: 'Moses and the prophets declare it was for the sin of the people. Moses declared that without the shedding of blood there is no remission of sin. Isaiah declared: **He was wounded for our transgressions; he was bruised for our iniquities; the chastisement of our peace was upon him; and with his stripes we are healed**. You ask me why the Messiah had to suffer. He suffered to pay the price of your sin.'

"The price of my sin? Then I began to see. It seemed as if scales were dropping from my eyes. JESUS shed his blood for me even as the sacrificial lamb upon the altar. His wounds on the cross were for my transgressions! He was bruised for my iniquities! Oh, the wonder of it all! - Just then we approached my home in Emmaus. We asked him to abide with us for it was toward evening and the day was far spent. To this he agreed.

"As he sat at meat with us, he took bread, and blessed it, and brake, and gave to us. Then suddenly our eyes were opened and we knew Him: and He vanished out of our sight. Luke cried out: 'It is the Lord, Cleopas! It is the Lord! He is risen. And, oh, **did not our hearts burn within us, while He talked with us by the way, and while He opened to us the Scriptures?'**

"Immediately we determined to return to Jerusalem to tell the apostles. We almost ran all the way. We found the eleven gathered together along with the others. Before we could say a word they cried to us, saying: '**The Lord is risen indeed, and hath appeared to Simon**.' Then Luke and I told our experience on our journey to Emmaus and how the Lord was known in the breaking of bread. How we rejoiced in the knowledge that JESUS was risen and is the Messiah. Yes, the Lord is risen. I walked with the risen Lord and knew it not. He opened the Scripture to us and I know now what a fool I was not to know that the Messiah had to suffer these things and thus enter into His glory. May the Lord open up the Scriptures to you; and then you, too, will walk with the risen Lord."

CHAPTER TWELVE "I Am A Sinner Saved By Grace" by Paul

"My name is Saul although now I am known as Paul. A change occurred in my life which was far more radical than the change in my name. Those who knew me in my youth and young manhood would consider that change almost unbelievable. It was a change as great as the difference between darkness and light. It can only be attributed to the power and grace of Almighty GOD. Truly I can testify that I am a sinner saved by grace.

"I was born in the city of Tarsus in the Province of Cilicia. Cilicia like all parts of the world at that time was under the control of the Romans. The population of Tarsus consisted chiefly of Greeks. There were of course Roman soldiers and government officials. And there was also a small number of Jews. Through a service rendered to the Roman Government my father became a Roman citizen. So I was free-born.

"Although a Roman citizen my father was a Hebrew of the Hebrews. He belonged to the strictest sect of our religion, namely, a Pharisee. It was his constant fear that his family might become contaminated with the idolatry and immorality of the Greeks and the Romans. We were strictly forbidden to take part in any of the pagan feasts and celebrations.

"My father, however, thought the best way of keeping us undefiled from idolatry was to teach us the tenets of our religion. Almost from an infant I was taught the stories of the Scriptures. The call of Abraham, the struggle between Jacob and Esau, Moses and the Passover, David and Goliath, and Daniel in the lion's den, were all familiar to me. We were taught to keep the law in all its legal aspects. I also learned about the Messiah who was to establish the Kingdom.

"As soon as I was old enough I was sent to the school connected with the synagogue. There I learned to read and write. At the synagogue we learned more about the law and the prophets. When visiting doctors of the law came to Tarsus we were allowed to hear their discussions and even allowed to ask questions.

"My father was not satisfied with the education that was possible in Tarsus and decided to send me to Jerusalem when I reached the age of ten. I can still remember my first glimpse of Jerusalem. I beheld the glittering roof of the Temple, the buildings on Mount Zion, and the ridge of Mount Olives rising high over all. As I passed through the gate of the Holy City I repeated the words of the Psalmist: '**I was glad when they said unto me, Let us go into the house of the Lord. Our feet shall stand within thy gates, O Jerusalem. Pray for the peace of Jerusalem: they shall prosper that love thee. Peace be within thy walls, and prosperity within thy palaces.**'

"I studied at the feet of one of the greatest of all the teachers of the Jews - Gamaliel. He was a man of integrity and wisdom. He was held in reputation of all the people. It was a privilege and an honour to learn from him. He was zealous for the law and for the honour of the Jewish nation. He taught us that only those who rigidly kept the law would live before the Holy GOD of Israel.

"Under the influence and teaching of Gamaliel I became a Pharisee of the Pharisees. It was our pride to keep even the most minute details of the law. My entire life was hemmed in by the law. I rigidly gave a tithe of everything which came into my possession. I fasted at least twice a week. I kept every holy day. My prayers were long and frequent. I kept the traditions concerning the washing of cups, pots, brazen vessels, and tables. I would not eat bread except that I washed my hands after the instructions of the elders. It was a tradition that water be poured over our closed hands so that the water might flow down to the elbows. Unless we washed in this manner we considered ourselves unclean. I lived in constant dread that I would break even one of the thousands of precepts which governed our lives. I wanted to be blameless in keeping of the law.

"Although I zealously kept all the externals of the law and the traditions there was one law which troubled me and that was the tenth commandment. This commandment taught us that we should not covet that which belonged to another. It was my besetting sin that I did covet. I coveted the influence and prominence of certain men. I coveted the wealth of others. I coveted the talents of others. I knew in this that I sinned against GOD. But I felt that my diligence in keeping all the details of the external laws more than made up for my failing in keeping the tenth commandment.

"Through the influence of Gamaliel I also became intensely patriotic. Along with others I felt that in order to keep our unity as a Jewish race we must exalt our religion. A political unity was not sufficient in our day because the Romans had crushed out our political life. We as Pharisees felt that above all things we must cling to the law and the religion of our fathers. Nothing must be allowed to interfere with our religion. Nothing must be permitted which would cause our people to despise the law. Nothing must be tolerated which would cast doubt upon the traditions. Above all things we the Jewish nation must cling to our religion and the law.

"You can well imagine the horror which I felt at something which occurred while I was absent from Judea. Upon finishing my schooling under Gamaliel I went back to visit my parents in Tarsus where I remained for several years. I did hear rumors about a certain JESUS who performed miracles and claimed to be the Messiah. This did not excite me as those who claimed to be the Messiah were many in the history of our nation. But evidently my friends in the city of Jerusalem took a more serious view of it for they influenced the Roman governor, Pilate, to crucify him. That would seem to finish the movement started by this JESUS.

"However, when I returned to Jerusalem I found things in a terrible state. It was claimed that this JESUS had risen from the dead for his tomb was found empty. A number of his followers claimed that they had seen him after his resurrection. One of his followers by the name of Peter had preached on the day of the feast of Pentecost and had succeeded in deceiving some three thousand who became followers of this supposed Messiah. And every day more joined this movement.

"I knew that something drastic had to be done immediately if this movement was to be stopped. The council had already thrown several into prison but they were released. I was somewhat disappointed in the counsel of my beloved teacher, Gamaliel. They had arrested the leading disciples of JESUS. To my mind they should have been put to death. But Gamaliel said: '**Refrain from these men, and let them alone: for if this counselor this work be of men, it will come to nought: but if it be of God, ye cannot overthrow it; lest haply ye be found even to fight against God.**'

"For all his wisdom Gamaliel did not see the danger and magnitude of this movement. He did not see that these followers of JESUS were out to destroy the law. They disregarded the Sabbath. They disregarded many rituals and set aside the traditions of the fathers. If they continued to grow and multiply they would destroy the unity of our race. I felt that they must be stopped at all cost. So I organized a number of faithful Pharisees to oppose this movement. The first thing we did was to compose a prayer to GOD. It was in these words that we prayed to GOD: 'Let there be no hope to them who apostatize from the true religion; and let heretics, how many soever they be, all perish as in a moment. And let the kingdom of pride be speedily rooted out and broken in our days. Blessed are thou, O Lord our God who destroyest the wicked, and bringest down the proud.'

"Prayer, however, was not enough. I determined to follow it up with action. I determined to destroy the church of JESUS of Nazareth. I led a mob into every home that honoured the name of JESUS. I caused them to be scourged. Many were cast into prison. If we caught them in the synagogue we had them publicly scourged. Some were put to death. I tried by torture to cause them to blaspheme the name of JESUS. Those who refused were terribly ill treated. As a result the movement was almost stamped out in Jerusalem. Hundreds fled out of the Holy City.

"But even this did not satisfy me. They propagated their heretical religion in distant parts. I was determined to persecute them to the ends of the world. I did this all for the glory of the GOD of Israel. There was one incident during my career as persecutor of the church which stood out. There was a man by the name of Stephen who tried to propagate this heretical religion in the synagogue of the Cilicians. I disputed with him to no avail. So we brought him to the council. Witnesses testified that Stephen spoke blasphemous words against the Temple and the Law. They said: '**We heard this Stephen say that Jesus of Nazareth shall destroy this place, and shall change the customs which Moses delivered us**.'

"The High Priest asked Stephen whether these things were so. Stephen related some of the history of our race. But he concluded by crying out against us: '**Ye stiffnecked and uncircumcised in heart and ears, ye do always resist the Holy Ghost: as your fathers did, so do ye. Which of the prophets have not your fathers persecuted? And they have slain them which shewed before of the coming of the Just One of whom ye have been now the betrayers and murderers; who have received the law by the disposition of angels, and have not kept it**.'

"Upon hearing this terrible accusation we cried out and gnashed upon him with our teeth. But he cried out: '**Behold, I see the heavens opened, and the Son of man standing on the right hand of God**.' Upon this we cried out with a loud voice and stopped our ears. We cast him out of the city and stoned him. Those who took part laid down their clothes at my feet. As the stones thudded against his body I remember him crying out: '**Lord Jesus, receive my spirit**.' And kneeling down he prayed: '**Lord, lay not this sin to their charge**.'

"I was more determined than ever to stamp out these followers of JESUS. Hearing that there were a number of them in Damascus I obtained letters to those in authority in the synagogue there. It was my plan to bring the followers of JESUS bound to Jerusalem. So I joined a caravan traveling to Damascus. As we neared the city suddenly there shone round about me a light from Heaven. I fell to the earth and heard a voice saying unto me, '**Saul, Saul, why persecutest thou me?**' And I said: '**Who art thou, Lord?**' And the Lord said, '**I am Jesus whom thou persecutest; it is hard for thee to kick against the pricks**.' This astonished me and I trembled like a leaf. I cried out: '**Lord, what wilt thou have me to do?**' And the Lord said unto me, '**Arise, and go into the city, and it shall be told thee what thou must do**.'

81

"I arose but I could not see. The men which were with me led me by the hand, and brought me into Damascus. I stayed at the house of one Judas, who lived on the street called Straight. For three days and nights I remained blind. I was not able to eat or drink. All that I could think about was my sin, my sin, my sin. I had persecuted the Son of the living GOD. In my mind I heard again the cries of those I had caused to be tortured. And in their cries I heard the voice of the Son of Man: '**Saul, Saul, why persecutest thou me?**' I heard the weeping of the women whom I had cast in prison. In the midst of their weeping I heard his voice: '**Saul, Saul, why persecutest thou me?**' And when I remembered how I had tried to make them blaspheme the Holy name of Him in whom they believed, I heard the voice: '**Saul, Saul, why persecutest thou me?**' I had persecuted the Son of the GOD whom I professed to love and serve.

"During the three days of darkness the face of Stephen came before me. I had encouraged vile men to stone him. They were actually stoning the Lord of Glory. '**Saul, Saul, why persecutest thou me?**' Would GOD ever forgive? Ah, Stephen had cried out: '**Lord, lay not this sin to their charge**.' Perhaps this prayer of Stephen would save me. I prayed and I prayed: 'GOD have mercy upon my guilty vile soul. GOD have mercy on me a sinner.'

"GOD did have mercy on me. JESUS appeared to one of His followers whose name was Ananias and directed him to come to me. As Ananias entered into my presence he put his hands upon me in tenderness and said: '**Brother Saul, the Lord, even Jesus, that appeared unto thee in the way as thou camest, hath sent me, that thou mightest receive thy sight, and be filled with the Holy Ghost**.' Upon that the scales fell from my eyes. Ananias baptized me. Now I experienced the blessing of salvation. The Lord forgave me a sinner. I was saved by His marvellous grace.

"As my voice reaches across the generations, it is my hope and prayer that all that hear might know that JESUS is both Lord and Saviour. He is the Messiah. There is none other name by which men can be saved. We cannot be justified by the keeping of the law. We can be justified only through faith in JESUS the CHRIST. As I once testified to the Philippian Jailor; '**Believe on the Lord Jesus Christ and thou shalt be saved and thy house**.'

CHAPTER THIRTEEN "GOD Gave Me No Convenient Season" by Antonius Felix

"My name is Antonius Felix. At one time my brother, Pallas, and I were slaves. But we were freed by Antonia the mother of Emperor Claudius. My brother Pallas was an attractive fellow and very clever. He became the favorite of Emperor Claudius and later of Emperor Nero. It was through the influence of my brother and Jonathan the high priest that I was appointed as procurator of Judea.

"My name is Felix. It means '*happy*.' But my name is a lie. I am miserable and live amongst the miserable. Through no great fault of my own I am a dweller in hell. I am condemned forever to a life of woe and misery. My soul is in torment. But here is an account of my life as procurator over the Province of Judea.

"My predecessor in office, Cumanus, was not very successful in keeping down the bands of robbers and assassins which roamed throughout Palestine. The Jews complained about him to the Emperor. Claudius removed him from office. Then through the influence of Jonathan the high priest of the Jews and also that of my brother Pallas, I was appointed to be governor over Judea.

"This fellow Jonathan, the high priest, thought that he could interfere with the way I governed simply because he helped in my appointment. I hated his interference. He thought that I should not accept gifts from those who came up before me for judgment. But why should I not profit from my office? It was the common practice of all judges to be influenced by gifts. Jonathan talked about justice but who in the Empire of Rome believed in justice? That high priest became troublesome because of his insistence, on justice. So I fixed him by bribing his best friend Doras to hire a band of robbers to assassinate him. This they did cleverly. They pretended they were going to worship GOD in the Temple. They had daggers under their garments. They plunged their daggers into

Jonathan. Then they mingled with the multitude and cried with them to catch the assassins. I used these clever fellows many times to murder my enemies, many of which were Jews whom I hated.

"Some of these assassins got too bold, particularly a chap by the name of Dineas. He was getting too rich in his plundering and I received nothing from him. I sent word to him if he would give himself up I would not punish him but allow him his freedom. The wretch believed me. As soon as he gave himself up I bound him in chains and sent him to Rome to be tried. This would make a good impression on the Emperor who would know how diligent I was in wiping out bands of robbers and assassins. Little did Claudius know I was using them for my own ends, although some of those sneaking Jews began to inform him.

"Though I despised the Jews yet I must confess I fell in love with a Jewess. She was the wife of Azizus, king of Emesa, a small kingdom in Syria. She was the most beautiful woman that I had ever seen. I forgot all my other loves. I was consumed with desire for her. I felt that she, too, loved me. What mattered if she were the wife of another? Why should we remain unhappy by the laws of any nation? Love is supreme. I had at this time a clever Jewish friend by the name of Simon a magician. I sent him to the court of Azizus. He persuaded Drusilla to leave her husband with the promise that she would receive great happiness. Surely it was better to be the wife of Felix, with all his influence in Rome, than to be the wife of an insignificant king.

"There were some Jews who said this was a transgression of the laws of their GOD. But why should two people remain unhappy all their lives just to keep some ancient laws which have no relationship to real life? It is happiness that counts.

"The Jews were having their own trouble about their religion. Some twenty or more years ago a man by the name of JESUS was crucified under Pilate. He really was not guilty of any crime but occasionally we have to please the Jews. I know that I do that every once in a while to keep them quiet. Well, it seems that the followers of this JESUS believe him to be the Messiah. They claim that he was resurrected from the dead and appeared to some of them. The

Jews were trying to stamp out this sect by sending them to prison and stoning others. It amused me to see the Jews fighting one another.

"I was curious about this sect after hearing so much about them. My wife, Drusilla, was also curious to know more about them. We had our opportunity of learning more when Captain Lysias in Jerusalem sent up a fellow by the name of Paul. He was the cause of a riot. It seems that he, too, was a follower of this JESUS and was one of the chief men of this sect.

"On the day of the trial the Jews had as their informer a certain orator by the name of Tertullus. He was a silver-tongued speaker and with great eloquence declaimed against Paul. But if he had used silver instead of oratory he might have made an impression on me. It is silver in which I am interested. Paul answered his arguments easily. I knew it was just a religious quarrel and that Paul had not done anything worthy of imprisonment. But there were two things in Paul's defense which interested me. The first was his declaration that he had come up to Jerusalem in order to bring alms and offerings to his nation. I figured out that the man must be rich and have rich friends. Immediately I made up my mind to keep him in prison until he offered me a large sum of money. I would make him pay well for his freedom.

"The second thing which interested me was the statement of Paul about a resurrection of the dead, both of the just and the unjust. He said that it was also a teaching of the law and prophets of the Jews. I have often wondered whether there was a life after death. We Romans had little regard for the gods and the teachings about them. It was all right for the ignorant masses. It kept them satisfied and quiet. But most of the nobles and ruling classes were skeptics. However, I could not help wondering whether there was a life after death.

"I asked Drusilla about this statement of Paul's regarding the resurrection of the just and unjust. She quoted a statement of one of the prophets of the Jews by the name of Daniel. He had written: **'And many of them that sleep in the dust of the earth shall awake, some to everlasting life, and some to shame and**

everlasting contempt.' Drusilla was also interested because she had heard about these followers of JESUS. We thought it might be interesting and amusing to hear this man Paul and at the same time I might discover the source of his wealth. So I summoned him to appear before Drusilla and myself.

"I commanded him to speak to us concerning this CHRIST and faith in him. Paul told us that

JESUS was the very Son of GOD and that He had lived with GOD throughout eternity. This JESUS was born of a virgin. Paul told us of some of the miracles which the CHRIST had performed. He told us of his crucifixion at the hands of the Jews and the Romans. But I already knew how Pilate had become mixed up in the death of this Jew. Then Paul told us of the resurrection of this JESUS the CHRIST. How he appeared to the apostles and how he appeared to him on his way to persecute the Christians.

"Then he told us a rather strange doctrine of how it was necessary to believe in this JESUS in order to receive the forgiveness of sin. This crucifixion was for the atonement of sin even though it was brought about by the hands of men. 'His blood,' said Paul, 'was shed for sin.' It was the same thing, he informed Drusilla, as the sacrifice in the Temple. This CHRIST was the sinoffering. But why should I, Felix, the procurator of Judea, be classified as a sinner? Why should I as Governor kneel as a sinner before this JESUS the CHRIST?

"Paul must have read my thoughts because he began to reason of righteousness, temperance, and judgment to come. He explained that righteousness was doing what was right towards man and towards GOD. He told me that lying was a sin against man and GOD. I always thought that lying was an accomplishment and I prided myself on my ability to deceive. Dishonesty was another sin, according to Paul. One should take no more than that to which he is entitled. I thought of the thousands of talents that I had appropriated from the public treasury and of all the plunder taken from the homes of the wealthy. Most of my wealth consisted of that which I took from others. If dishonesty is a sin my sin would be enormous.

87

"Then he mentioned injustice and murder. I always considered it right to receive gifts which he termed bribes. But he told me that his GOD considered the taking of bribes as something particularly abhorrent. His GOD hated injustice. And as for murder Paul said that the murderer would never enter into Heaven, the abode of the righteous. I had tortured and murdered hundreds. Often for no great reason I ordered my soldiers to kill and plunder. No murderer would enter into Heaven, said Paul.

"My conscience was pricked because I knew that I lied, stole, was unjust and a murderer. But why should I be troubled in conscience? Why should I, Antonius Felix, worry about what this religious fanatic calls transgressions of the law of GOD? Why must I be righteous? But again that Paul seemed to read my thoughts. He declared that the living GOD was righteous and demands that all His creatures be righteous. This GOD had said: '**Be ye holy as I am holy**.' This Holy GOD would not tolerate wickedness in the lives of His creatures. He commands all to do what is right. I had never thought of GOD as such a holy Being and one who demanded righteousness. This thought began to trouble me.

"Then this persistent disciple of CHRIST continued digging at my conscience. He spoke of temperance. I had been everything but a temperate man. I have never tried to bridle my passions. Eat, drink, and be merry has been my philosophy as that of many others. Paul mentioned adultery. Drusilla turned crimson and I felt uncomfortable.

I thought it had been clever to take her away from her husband. But now my conscience began to burn. The fellow made me squirm as he revealed the law of his GOD against adultery and sexual lusts. Then the thought struck me that his GOD had not showed His displeasure. I had experienced no drastic punishment. I held a place of honour. I was becoming wealthy. And in Drusilla I had my heart's desire. This GOD of Paul's could not be so hard against sin.

"But Paul struck terror into my heart by speaking of the judgment. He told me that GOD did not always punish upon earth but that there was to be a final judgment. At that final judgment all our deeds would be shown and even our thoughts. I thought of my lies.

I thought of my curses. I thought of my stealing. I thought of my injustices. I thought of my murders. And I thought of my lusts. What a record to present in front of the holy and righteous GOD! What would He do? Paul told me. He told me that GOD would separate the good from the wicked. He repeated these words of CHRIST: '**Then shall he say also unto them on the left, Depart from me, ye cursed, into the eternal fire which is prepared for the devil and his angels**.' When he spoke of hell fire and eternal punishment I trembled like a leaf.

"Paul observed this and said: 'You are trembling and well you might. You are a guilty sinner and under the condemnation of the righteous GOD. You have but one chance and that is to repent and turn to CHRIST. Believe that He died upon the cross for your sins and you will be forgiven. Though your sins are as crimson they shall be as white as snow. CHRIST will give you strength to live a holy life. Repent and believe on the Lord JESUS CHRIST:

"I pondered that offer of forgiveness through faith in CHRIST for a few moments. It would be wonderful to know that all my sins were forgiven and that GOD would receive me into His Heaven. But to repent! That would mean leaving Drusilla. Would that be a fair thing for me to do after taking her from her husband? To repent! That would mean to restore what I had stolen! I was just becoming rich and I needed money. To repent and become a follower of the CHRIST! Why the Jews would hate me even more and they would try to influence Claudius to remove me.

It might mean the loss of this influential position. This would be no time to repent and become a Christian. I would wait for a more convenient season. And so I cried out to Paul: '**Go thy way for this time; when I have a convenient season, I will call for thee**.'

"A more convenient season! GOD never gave me a convenient season. I became fonder of Drusilla as time went on. A son was born to us. How would it be possible for me to leave her? The times became more difficult to rule. There was a battle between the Jews and the Syrians. Just because my soldiers plundered some of the rich Jews they complained to Nero who had succeeded Claudius as Emperor. My brother Pallas did what he could but I was recalled to Rome. Certainly it was not convenient to turn to CHRIST when my position and life were at stake. That was not a convenient season. Why did GOD allow my enemies to triumph if He wanted me to repent? Why did He take away the position through which I accumulated wealth?

"Nero would not re-appoint me to Judea. He said that he would not displease certain influential Jews. Naturally I had to spend all my time to get some other kind of appointment. And that was not easy because Nero thought I had failed and he was a cruel man. With all my worries it certainly was not time to repent and become a Christian. That would spoil all my chances. The season was not convenient.

"However, there was still the thought in my mind that I would repent, perhaps, when I was about to die. That would be a convenient time to prepare for the other world and the terrible judgment to come. Death approached and how I fought him. Do you know what it is to fight death? It takes your every breath and every ounce of strength. You have no time to think. You have no time to repent. All you think of is that you want to live. And, yes, if GOD will let you live then you will repent. I fought with death. It was a terrible struggle. I thought I would win. But death conquered and I awoke in hell. GOD did not give me a convenient season.

"A more convenient season! That is the thought that torments me day after day, week after week, year after year, century after century. A more convenient season! That is the flame that cannot be extinguished in this endless time. A more convenient season! That is the worm that dieth not in this eternal hell. If GOD had only given me a convenient season. If GOD had only given me a convenient season - a more convenient season. O that that thought might be extinguished and that that worm might die! A more convenient season. GOD never gave me a more convenient season. I am damned throughout eternity with that timeless flame and deathless worm. A more convenient season! GOD never gave me a more convenient season."

CHAPTER FOURTEEN "I Was Awakened By An Earthquake" by the Philippian Jailor

"I have a most remarkable experience to relate to you. I was awakened by an earthquake. This may not seem unusual unless you realize that it was not that of ordinary sleep from which I was awakened but a sleep of death. This earthquake caused me to enter into a world which I never knew existed. But let me tell you my story in order.

"I was a Roman living in the colony city of Philippi in Macedonia. My occupation was that of jailor. I was proud of my position which was a very important one. The malefactors were many. Our prison was large. Not only was my position important but it was a very responsible one. It was our Roman law that if the jailor allowed any criminal to escape that he himself had to bear whatever punishment was due this criminal. If I allowed one to escape who was to receive the death penalty then I myself would have to die in his place. So you can see what a responsible position this was. It was my pride, however, that not one prisoner had escaped. I saw to it that every one was chained or fastened in stocks. I thoroughly checked each of the doors and the locks which fastened the door. I made certain that no prisoner escaped. Indeed, my life depended upon it.

"The City of Philippi in which I lived was one of which we were proud. We sought in all its activities to make it like Rome the capital city of the Empire. Roman law and Roman customs held sway over our city. We came into prominence when Anthony defeated Brutus and Cassius near our city. Brutus committed suicide and Cassius ordered his freedman to slay him. In this they proved themselves honorable and true Romans. It was our belief that in the time of defeat it was both honorable and brave to take one's life.

"The citizens of Philippi had great respect for Apollo, the GOD of prophecy. Many journeyed to Delphi, the oracle of Apollo. It was there that Apollo killed Python the serpent which guarded the oracle. It was for this that Apollo was sometimes called Pythius, and the Delphi was formerly called Pythia. The priestesses of the oracle were possessed of the spirit of Python and were enabled to disclose secrets and forecast future events. Within our city were many fortune tellers and soothsayers. Many of our citizens would consult a soothsayer about every venture in which they were to partake.

"Our city had a very famous diviner in the person of a young slave girl. She was truly possessed of the spirit of Python and was equal to any priestess of the Delphi. While I had not consulted her personally because of the pressure of my work, many of my friends had. One friend told me how she had prophesied that a ship in which he was interested would be wrecked but that his uncle who was aboard ship would be saved. And this actually happened. Another friend told how she had told him that within ten days he would receive a large fortune. And this actually occurred. I could tell you of one event after another that she truly prophesied would occur.

"She was owned by a group of men who were becoming immensely rich through her divination. The citizens flocked to consult her. As a matter of fact she became so busy that one had to make an appointment weeks ahead of time. She brought her owners much gain.

"Then something happened. It seems that several Jews had entered into our city. There were not many Jews living in Philippi. There were a few. They worshipped on what they called their Sabbath by the river side. But these Jews were strangers. And the remarkable thing was that this young girl who had the spirit of Python within her began to follow these strangers. She did not follow them silently but cried out: **'These men are the servants of the most high God, which shew unto us the way of salvation: People told me that she followed these Jews wherever they went. From early morning till they retired at night she followed them. And**

92

constantly she cried out: 'These men are the servants of the most high God, which shew unto us the way of salvation.'

"The men who owned her were at their wits end. She refused to prophesy. They could do nothing with her. They tried to persuade her to prophesy as formerly. But she refused. It seemed as though she were in a trance and that the spirit of Python compelled her to follow these men and to cry out: '**These men are the servants of the most high God, which shew unto us the way of salvation.**' The whole city was stirred up about this and it was all that my friends talked about.

"Then another unusual thing happened. The leader of these Jews suddenly pronounced these words to the spirit of Python within her: '**I command thee in the name of Jesus Christ to come out of her.**' And the spirit left her. The owners of this girl were dumfounded. They tried to have her prophesy. But she no longer had the ability. She was just like any normal girl. This meant they would no longer be able to profit from her. They filled the air with their curses.

"They caught up with two of these Jews whose names were Paul and Silas. They dragged them into the market place before the magistrates. A large crowd followed them to see the excitement. The owners of the girl said to the magistrates: '**These men, being Jews, do exceedingly trouble our city, and teach customs, which are not lawful for to receive, neither to observe, being Romans.**'

"Both the multitude and the magistrates were indignant when they heard the nationality of these men. These Jews had just stirred up trouble in Rome so that Emperor Claudius expelled them. And now they were stirring up trouble in our city. And it was a Roman law that a foreign religion could not be introduced. It was told that these Jews spoke about another GOD of whom we knew nothing. Were not our gods sufficient without introducing a strange deity? As a colony of Rome we must be faithful to the laws of Rome. So reasoned the magistrates.

"The magistrates tore the clothing off this Paul and Silas and ordered them to be beaten with rods. This was no pleasant thing, let me tell you. I have seen prisoners more dead than alive after such a beating. Many would have their bones broken and flesh lacerated. After these two Jews were thoroughly beaten they were brought to me. The magistrates gave me strict instructions to keep them safely or else I would receive what they received and more.

"You may be well assured that I would be obedient to the order of the magistrates. I took them into the innermost dungeon. This we kept for the most vicious prisoners. I hated to enter into this dungeon myself for it was cold and damp. It was always annoying to have the chains rust on the bodies of the prisoners. We kept several stocks there into which we fastened the feet of the criminals. This prohibited them from lying down and if torture were ordered, we could stretch their limbs. Besides being cold and damp it was overrun with vermin.

"The bodies of the two Jews were raw and bleeding. Those who used the rods had done a good job. The two men were strangely meek and silent. I was accustomed to have men struggle and curse. But I had no difficulty with them at all. I was curious about them for I knew of their power to cast the spirit of Python out of the slave girl. And I knew what she said about them that they were servants of the most high GOD who do shew the way of salvation.

"When I had them safely fastened in the stocks I could not help mocking them. I said: 'So you are the fellows that are the servants of the most high GOD. Well, your GOD could not have been so powerful or else you would not have been beaten and imprisoned. And you are going to proclaim the way of salvation! You better try and save yourselves. No one has been able to loose himself from these stocks and chains. And look at those powerful doors. Who could burst them open? You Jews and your most high GOD! Go ahead and proclaim your way of salvation!' They said nothing but their lips moved as though they were making some petition of their GOD. So I left them.

"After making certain that all the doors were properly fastened I retired for the night and slept. Suddenly at midnight I was flung out of my bed by a mighty upheaval. It was an earthquake. My first thought was my prisoners. I ran out and behold the doors that I had fastened so thoroughly were all wide open and all the prisoners must have fled. What could I do? I would have to answer with my life. I could not stand the disgrace. So as a Roman and like Brutus I drew out my sword from its sheath. I was just about to plunge it into my heart when the sound of a voice came from the innermost dungeon: '**Do thyself no harm; for we are all here**.'

"Could that be true? I called for a light. I sprang into the inner dungeon and behold there were the two Jews free from the stocks and chains. They must be superhuman. I fell trembling before them and then I led them out of the prison.

"It is somewhat hard for me to relate all the thoughts that entered into my mind. But I never was more frightened in all my life. I suddenly realized that the GOD of these strangers was the living GOD. The earthquake, the opening of the prison doors, the safety of all the prisoners made me realize the GOD of these two Jews was both almighty and living. Almost I had plunged myself into the presence of the living GOD by an act of suicide. And I had insulted GOD. I mocked Him and His messengers. All my life I had lived indifferent to GOD and even cursed His name. I denied His existence. My conscience smote me and I trembled as a leaf.

"As soon as I led the two men out of prison I fell down before them and cried out: '**Sirs what must I do to be saved?**' I knew that they had the way of salvation. I knew that they could direct me as to what I must do so that the wrath of GOD would not fall upon me. Whatever they said I would do. It mattered not if I had to give up all my silver and gold. It mattered not how many sacrifices I would have to offer to their GOD. It mattered not what penance they might prescribe.

I was ready to do anything so that the wrath of almighty GOD would not come upon me. Trembling I waited for their directions.

"Then they told me what is surely the most wonderful news that this world has ever heard. They said, '**Believe on the Lord Jesus Christ, and thou shalt be saved, and thy house**.' I did not know who this JESUS CHRIST was nor what it was to believe on him. So they explained what they meant not only to me but to my household also who had gathered around us.

"They said that JESUS CHRIST was the Son of the GOD whom I had offended and whose wrath I feared. They told me that the Son of GOD entered into our flesh by being born of a virgin in a little town of Bethlehem in Palestine. He lived in the country of the Jews and at the age of thirty began to teach the message of the kingdom of GOD. They told me of the many miracles which He accomplished and how He forgave men their sins. And then they told me how this Son of GOD was crucified upon a cross like a common criminal.

"'But', said Paul, 'our message does not stop with a crucified JESUS. He rose from the tomb on the third day and was seen of the disciples. He appeared to me and told me to proclaim the way of salvation to the Gentiles even as the slave girl intimated. That is why Silas and I are here in the city of Philippi. You ask us what you must do in order to be saved. In one respect it is not necessary to do anything for by the works of the law no one is justified. The reason why it is not necessary for you to do anything is because CHRIST has done it for you. When He died upon the cross He took our sins upon Him. You are still trembling because you realize that all your life you have ignored the true and living GOD. You cannot atone for such a sin. But JESUS, the Son of GOD, has taken your sin upon Himself. He died for you. The thing which you have to do is to believe in our Lord JESUS. You must believe that He died for your sins upon the cross. '**Believe on the Lord Jesus Christ and thou shalt be saved**.'

"Did I believe? Of course I believed. It was the most wonderful news I had ever heard. It was wonderful to know that GOD loved me so much as to give His only begotten Son and that by simply believing on Him my sins were forgiven. My wife and my children also believed. I washed the wounds of Silas and Paul. And even before the day dawned we were all baptized.

"It took an earthquake to awaken me from my sleep of death. I tremble to think what would have happened if GOD had not sent an earthquake. I would have remained a lost and condemned sinner. And to think that there are thousands who live as I lived, utterly indifferent to the fact that there is a living GOD in Heaven. They mock Him and curse Him. But the living GOD cannot be mocked. He will punish. Many scoff at the message of salvation which He sends by His messengers. They are scoffing the living and mighty GOD. Oh, that they might awake before it is too late! Oh, that their conscience might become alive to the danger of falling into the hands of an angry GOD! But I am afraid that it will take an earthquake to awaken many to their danger.

"It is my hope and prayer that my testimony may be used of GOD to awaken those who are sleeping the sleep of death. If your conscience is awakened I bring to you the message of the Gospel: '**Believe on the Lord Jesus Christ and thou shalt be saved and thy house.**'

CHAPTER FIFTEEN "From Pagan To Christian" by Cornelius

"I have the proud distinction of being the first Gentile received into the Christian Church. In me began the fulfillment of the promise that light would be given to the Gentiles. It is not to be wondered at that my experience and that of my friends who were with me was somewhat unusual. We spoke with tongues even as did the disciples upon the day of Pentecost when the Holy Spirit fell upon them. This was to signal the acceptance of the Gentiles into the Church of CHRIST. Of speaking in tongues, however, I do not glory as much as I do that in CHRIST I found my Saviour and One who satisfied the deep hunger and thirst of my soul.

"My name is Cornelius. No name was more honorable in Rome than that of the Cornelian House. My parents constantly impressed upon me to uphold the honour of our family name. My parents were considered to be very old fashioned because they still believed in the old Roman virtues of honesty, keeping one's oath, chastity, and faithfulness to the marriage relationship. All this was out of style in my day and generation. This was due to the Grecian influence. Although we conquered the Greeks yet they conquered us with their infidelity and frivolity.

"It was due to my parents that I took a more serious view of life. Then sensuality, drunkenness, and immorality that was rife in Rome disgusted me. There was something within me which could take no enjoyment in the debaucheries that were so prevalent in Rome. I longed for something better. My soul seemed hungry for truth and virtue.

"I began a search for something which would satisfy the hunger of my soul. Early in life I realized that the worship of Roman gods was a farce. We had many gods. Every phase of life was controlled by some god. There was the god of the field, the god of the pasture, the god of sowing, the god of harvest, and the god of the fruit. We even had a god by the name of Juno Unxia whose work was to anoint the door-hinges at weddings. For a while I sought to appease these gods by prayers, penances, and sacrifices. But I found no satisfaction for my soul. I felt that the gods were not real. In common with the ruling classes and the intellectuals of our day we often went through a form of worship of these gods for we thought it was a good way to keep the masses quiet but we did not believe in them.

"Some of my friends in Rome turned to the philosophy of Epicurus. According to this philosopher the great evil that afflicted men was fear: fear of the gods and fear of death. His aim was to get rid of these fears. He taught that the gods have nothing to do with the affairs of men and thus not to be feared. He taught that death meant the end of our existence and thus not to be feared. The chief aim of life was pleasure.

"This type of teaching appealed to many. But I could not rid my soul of the thought that I was responsible to some god. Something within me convinced me that there were supernatural beings to whom an account of life had to be made. I could not rid my soul of the fear of some unknown god or gods. Also I felt that my soul was immortal. There was a life beyond this life. The philosophy of Epicurus could not satisfy the hunger and thirst of my soul.

"Stoicism had a greater appeal to me and to many other Romans. It sought to crush the evil passions of the soul. But in so doing it seemed to crush the soul itself. Not only evil passions but natural affections, such as love for family, were to be obliterated. Many of the stoics did not believe in the immortality of the soul. The god of the stoic did not seem to be a personal god but the universe. This philosophy left my soul cold. There was still that feeling of dissatisfaction. The hunger and thirst of my soul were still present.

"It was while I was under the influence of stoicism that I sought a career in the army of the Empire. Fame seemed to be the highest aim of life. By military exploits I would again bring glory to the name of Cornelius. So I became a centurion over a cohort. My company was sent to Palestine to keep the country of the Jews in order. We were stationed in Caesarea wherein was the residence of the Procurator. My wife and children accompanied me.

"In Caesarea I came in contact with the Jews and their religion. My first contact was not pleasant. The Jews hated us Romans. Of course, it is understandable that a conquered nation should hate those who conquered them. But never have I witnessed such bitter hatred. Gradually, however, I won a few friends amongst the Jews but even they acted strangely. I befriended a certain Jew and did him a real service. He seemed very grateful. I asked him to have dinner with me at my home. But he seemed shocked at the thought of dining with me and refused. I learned later that it was part of their religion to have no dealings with Gentiles. It was alright to do business with us but there was to be no social relationships.

"There were several who told me about their religion. I was fascinated by their conception of GOD. There was but one GOD who ruled over the world. He was the Creator of the world. We were His creatures. What interested me was that this GOD did not have the weaknesses of our gods. He was righteous and holy. He would not tolerate evil. He had the power to deliver His people. There was no material form to this GOD; He was a spirit. He had revealed Himself and His will to certain prophets.

"I came under the conviction that the GOD of the Jews was the true GOD. He satisfied my soul more than any god or any philosophy. I began to pray to Him and taught my family also to worship Him. But there were certain things about the Jewish religion which brought doubt in my heart: not concerning their GOD but their manner of worship. I went up with the Procurator to Jerusalem and observed the worship in the Temple of the Jews. It seemed like a business to me.

There was the selling of sacrifices and exchanging of money. I was disappointed because I expected a high type of worship - something different than the worship at the temples of Roman gods.

"When I arrived back at Caesarea I told my Jewish friends of my disappointment. They told me of their expectations of the Messiah who would teach them all things. GOD had promised to send them one greater than Moses who would instruct them in all things. This reminded me of the rumors I had heard concerning a man by the name of JESUS. As a matter of fact, I heard about him from a fellow officer who was stationed in Jerusalem. He had charge of the crucifixion of this JESUS.

"He told me about the trial of JESUS before Pilate. It seems that JESUS claimed to be the Messiah and the Son of GOD. The Jews felt that this was blasphemy and according to their laws he should be stoned to death. Pilate yielded to their wishes and condemned the man to be crucified although his heart was not in it. Pilate gave JESUS into the charge of my friend who also was a centurion. Some of the rougher element of his soldiers scourged JESUS and played with him. They had heard that the Jews refused to acknowledge that JESUS was their king so they thought they would make him a king in mockery. They placed a crown of thorns upon him and mockingly worshipped him as king.

"Then my friend told me about the crucifixion. He told me that things proceeded about as usual until noonday. Then darkness came over the land. This remained for three hours. He then heard this JESUS cry out with a loud voice and suddenly the earth did quake and rocks were split. Graves were opened and it was reported that the bodies of the dead were seen. This sent fear into the heart of my friend and he felt that this JESUS truly was the Son of the GOD of the Jews. Later it was reported that this JESUS rose from the tomb.

"Whatever all this meant I continued my prayers to GOD. My soul was not entirely satisfied. I felt that there was something lacking in my relationship to GOD. I felt so unworthy and guilty before Him. But while I was praying about the ninth hour of the day, an angel of GOD appeared to me. Fear entered into my heart and I said: '**What is it, Lord?**' And he said to me: '**Thy prayers and thine alms are come up for a memorial before God. And now send men to Joppa, and call for one Simon, whose surname is Peter: he lodgeth with one Simon a tanner, whose house is by the sea side: he shall tell thee what thou oughtest to do.**'

"This vision filled my heart with joy. At last I would know the truth. At last my soul would be satisfied. Oh that this Peter might come speedily and reveal unto me the will of the living GOD. I called two of my servants and a devout soldier and sent them to Joppa even as the angel told me. While they went I called my kinsmen and close friends. They became as excited as I for many longed to know the truth concerning GOD.

"Several days later Peter came along with some of his friends. When I realized that here was a man of GOD who had a message for me from GOD, I fell down at his feet and worshipped him. But he wanted no worship. He took me up and said: '**Stand up; I myself also am a man**.' Then he said to us: '**Ye know how that it is an unlawful thing for a man that is a Jew to keep company or come unto one of another nation; but God hath shewed me that I should not call any man common or unclean. Therefore came I unto you without gainsaying, as soon as I was sent for: I ask therefore for what intent ye have sent for me?**'

"I answered: '**Four days ago I was fasting until this hour; and at the ninth hour I prayed in my house, and, behold, a man stood before me in bright clothing, and said, Cornelius, thy prayer is heard, and thine alms are had in remembrance in the sight of God. Send therefore to Joppa, and call hither Simon, whose surname is Peter; he is lodged in the house of one Simon a tanner by the sea side: who, when he cometh, shall speak unto thee. Immediately therefore I sent to thee; and thou hast well done that thou art come. Now therefore are we all here present before God, to hear all things that are commanded thee of God.**'

"Peter replied with his message from GOD. He said: '**Of a truth I perceive that God is no respecter of persons: but in every nation he that feareth him, and worketh righteousness, is accepted with him. The word which God sent unto the children of Israel, preaching peace by Jesus Christ: (He is Lord of all:) that word, I say, ye know, which was published throughout all Judea, and began from Galilee, after the baptism which John preached; how God anointed Jesus of Nazareth with the Holy Ghost and with power: who went about doing good, and healing all that were oppressed of the devil; for God was with him. And we are witnesses of all things which he did both in the land of the Jews, and in Jerusalem; whom they slew and hanged on a tree: Him God raised up the third day, and shewed him openly;**

not to all the people, but unto witnesses chosen before of God, even to us, who did eat and drink with him after he rose from the dead. And he commanded us to preach unto the people, and to testify that it is he which was ordained of God to be the Judge of the quick and the dead. To him give all the prophets witness, that through his name whosoever believeth in him shall receive remission of sins.'

"At this point the Holy Spirit came upon us. We believed the message of salvation. We believed on the name of the Lord JESUS CHRIST. We believed that through His name we received the remission of sin. The Holy Spirit enabled us to speak with tongues to magnify the living GOD who was so gracious in sending His messenger to us with the good news of salvation.

"This astonished the friends of Peter. They never expected that the Holy Spirit would be given to the Gentiles. But Peter said: '**Can any man forbid water, that these should not be baptized, which have received the Holy Spirit as well as we?**' Then we who believed were baptized.

"Never have I ceased praising GOD for the blessing of salvation. It is a matter of joy to me that I was the first Gentile to enter in the Christian Church. But of greater joy was the realization that the door of the Church was open to all Gentiles. The partition between Jew and Gentile has been broken down through the blood of CHRIST. In CHRIST there is neither Roman nor Jew, Barbarian nor Greek, bond nor free. We are one body in Christ JESUS.

"It was also a matter of joy to me that we Romans received a special gift of the Holy Spirit in that we spoke with tongues - a sign that the Gospel key had been used to open the door to the Gentiles, and as a sign to the Jews. The gracious Lord thus indicated to the believing Jews, who found it so difficult to leave their prejudice against Gentiles, that we, too, were acceptable to the Lord and could receive the promises. That was a matter of greater rejoicing.

"But my greatest joy was that GOD revealed JESUS CHRIST to my soul as Lord and Saviour. Now I testify that my soul is satisfied. I have peace with GOD. I found no satisfaction in the gods of the

103

Romans or the Greeks. I found no satisfaction in the various philosophies of our day. CHRIST and CHRIST alone satisfied my soul.

"Now if it chance that my voice reaches those who are groping for truth, seeking for soul satisfaction, and longing for peace with the living GOD: let me point you to the CHRIST even as Peter pointed Him out to me. In His name and in His name alone is there remission of sin and reconciliation with the true GOD. May GOD by His Holy Spirit reveal the CHRIST to your soul."

CHAPTER SIXTEEN "I Was Almost Persuaded To Be A Christian" by King Herod Agrippa II

"To my mind there is no more terrible word than the word almost. It is a word that sears with greater intensity than a literal flame. Would that the pain of hell were only a burning body, as well as a burning conscience! Would that I could escape from that burning flame almost! It torments me day and night. It is an everlasting flame of torment.

"It is the word almost that made me a dweller in hell. It is a cursed word. Almost made the difference between Heaven and hell. Almost made the difference between everlasting happiness and eternal misery. Almost made the difference between the love of GOD and the wrath of GOD. It is a tormenting word. Almost I was in the arms of CHRIST but I continued in the clutches of the devil. Almost my sins were pardoned but I continued in the guilt of sin. Almost I ascended into Heaven but I descended into hell. Better had my tongue been burned before uttering that word almost. Now it remains with me to torture and torment. It is a hellish flame.

"It came about in this way. On earth I was known as King Herod Agrippa II. I was the greatgrandson of Herod the Great who ruled when JESUS was born in Bethlehem. My father, Agrippa I, favoured the cause of Judaism over against Christianity. He slew James the apostle with a sword. I was sent to Rome for my education. I lived in the palace of Emperor Claudius who personally saw to my education.

"Although I was taught to worship the Roman deities my heart leaned to the religion of the Jews. As a matter of fact I was circumcised and studied the law and the prophets. While in Rome I secured several favours for the Jews. I persuaded Claudius to relinquish the official high-priestly robes which the Romans had taken from the Jews. I often represented the cause of the Jews at court.

"My father died when I was seventeen. Claudius thought I was too young to rule over Judea .. But when my uncle, Herod of Chalcis, died I was given his domain. The people there called me king. However, at the age of twenty-five Claudius gave me the tetrarchies of Philip and Lysanias so that I became a king in reality. Sometime later Emperor Nero added a number of cities to my domain.

"Perhaps you know something about my sisters, Drusilla and Bernice, who were somewhat notorious in my day. Drusilla left her husband in order to live with Felix. Concerning my sister Bernice I would prefer to say nothing. We lived together in such a way that it caused a scandal to both Jews and Romans. We were severely criticized. So much were we criticized that Bernice married King Polemo of Sicily. But she soon left him and came back to me. Before you condemn me too much you must realize that she was unusually attractive. Afterwards she became the mistress of Emperor Vespasian and also Emperor Titus his son.

"You might think by this scandal in my life that I was irreligious. That is not so. I was intensely interested in all religious questions. Early I became convinced that the Jewish religion was far superior to the paganism of Rome. I believed in the existence of the GOD of the Jews. I embraced their religion and was circumcised. The writings of the Prophets interested me a great deal. Of course, I became acquainted with the promise of the Messiah. This Messiah, according to the Prophets, would establish a great Kingdom. This Kingdom would rule over all the nations of the earth.

"In the history of the Jewish nation many claimed to be this promised Messiah. The most recent one was a man by the name of JESUS who was born when my great-grandfather, Herod the Great, was ruling. Nothing came of his claims, however, as he was crucified under Pilate. His followers claimed that he had risen from the tomb on the third day after his crucifixion. It was claimed that he appeared to many of his disciples. According to the Jewish religion and the teachings of the Prophets a resurrection was possible. This phase of it interested me very much.

"Whereas it was thought that this movement would die out, it seemed to increase. The followers of JESUS, who were called

Christians, were terribly persecuted. My father took the side of the Jews against the Christians and to please them he slew James the apostle. I myself had not contacted this movement but was very much interested in it. My opportunity to know more about it came during a visit Bernice and I made to Caesarea to pay our respects to Festus who had succeeded Felix as procurator over Judea.

"Festus was in a quandary about what to do with a famous prisoner by the name of Paul. He told me that his accusers brought no accusation of evil-doing except in regard to the question of religion. He said that the main question seemed to be about one JESUS whom the Jews said was dead but whom Paul maintained was alive. I had heard about this Paul who at one time persecuted the Christians himself but who had become the leader of the Christians. I said to Festus that I would like to hear this man. So Festus said we would hear him on the morrow.

"Bernice was also interested in hearing this Paul and made me promise that I would take her along. Many called her the most wicked woman of our generation. But, as in my case, she was not irreligious. When she married King Polemo she made him embrace the Jewish religion. She was interested in anything that affected Judaism.

"When the time came the prisoner Paul stood before us in his chains. I said: '**Thou art permitted to speak for thyself**.' Then Paul gave his defense. I must confess that his words gripped me. He spoke with sincerity. Somehow I felt that he was speaking the truth. His experience was real.

He started by telling how he belonged at first to the straitest sect of the Jews, the Pharisees. He said it was concerning the hope of Israel that he was judged. That hope, of course, was the coming of the Messiah. And he asked me whether I thought it incredible that GOD should raise the dead. Of course, it was not incredible as GOD had performed many miracles throughout the history of the Jewish nation. GOD could raise the dead. This I acknowledged within my heart.

"Then he told us how he had persecuted the Christians at Jerusalem - how he imprisoned some and caused others to be put to death. But let me give you the remaining part of Paul's defense in his own words so that you might have some idea of how it impressed me. Paul continued: '**And I punished them oft in every synagogue, and compelled them to blaspheme; and being exceedingly mad against them, I persecuted them even unto strange cities. Whereupon as I went to Damascus with authority and commission from the chief priests, at midday, O King, I saw in the way a light from Heaven; above the brightness of the sun, shining round about me and them which journeyed with me. And when we were all fallen to the earth, I heard a voice speaking unto me, and saying in the Hebrew tongue, Saul, Saul, why persecutest thou me? It is hard for thee to kick against the pricks. And I said, Who art thou, Lord? He answered: I am Jesus whom thou persecutest. But rise, and stand upon thy feet: for I have appeared unto thee for this purpose, to make thee a minister and a witness both of these things which thou hast seen, and of those things in the which I will appear unto thee; delivering thee from the people, and from the Gentiles, unto whom now I send thee, to open their eyes, and to turn them from darkness to light, and from the power of Satan unto God, that they may receive forgiveness of sins, and inheritance among them which are sanctified by faith that is in me. Whereupon, a king Agrippa, I was not disobedient unto the heavenly vision: but shewed first unto them at Damascus, and at Jerusalem, and throughout all the coasts of Judea, and then to the Gentiles, that they should repent and turn to God, and do works meet for repentance. For these causes the Jews caught me in the temple, and went about to kill me. Having therefore obtained help of God, I continue unto this day, witnessing both to small and great, saying none other things than those which the prophets and Moses did say should come: that Christ, should suffer, and that he should be the first that should rise from the dead, and should shew light unto the people, and to the Gentiles.'**

"At this time there was a sudden interruption. Festus, my fellow judge, could not contain himself. He cried out: '**Paul, thou art**

beside thyself; much learning doth make thee mad.' I can understand why Festus would think that Paul was out of his mind. To his pagan mind the talk about the resurrection of JESUS, of repentance, and of forgiveness of sin would sound like the ravings of a mad man. I had, however, a better understanding of these things through my study of the Prophets. I knew the power of GOD. I knew what the teaching of repentance meant. I understood that atonement had to be made for sins. But this was all a foreign language to Festus who considered that much learning had made Paul mad.

"Paul replied by stating to Festus: '**I am not mad, most noble Festus; but speak forth the words of truth and soberness. For the king knoweth of these things, before whom also I speak freely: for I am persuaded that none of these things are hidden from him; for this thing was not done in a corner**.' And then Paul turned to me and said: '**King Agrippa, believest thou the prophets? I know that thou believest**.'

"Yes, I believed the Prophets. I believed in their teachings of the coming of the Messiah. I believed in their doctrine of the resurrection. I knew it was necessary to repent in order to please GOD as the Prophets stated so frequently. I knew that one had to obtain the forgiveness of sin before one could stand in the presence of the holy GOD of Israel. And now Paul was challenging me to believe that JESUS was the Messiah. This meant repentance and turning to JESUS for forgiveness.

"There was something compelling about the words of the prisoner Paul. His earnestness and sincerity impressed me. I felt that he was telling the truth about the Messiah. But for me to believe in this JESUS and to become his follower was something quite difficult. It would mean the opposition of the Jews whose friendship I prized. It would mean that they would turn against me even as they turned against Paul. Why, I might even be put in chains like Paul and lose my position as King. I would lose my friends for they would think I had lost my mind. No, I will not be persuaded to believe in this JESUS. It is too risky. It demands too much.

"I had not lost what Paul said about repentance. He stated that one had to repent his sins. While I loved the religion of the Jews I lived the life of the Romans. According to Paul one had to turn away from sin before one could become a follower of JESUS and receive the forgiveness of sin. That would mean that I would have to give up Bernice. It would mean that I would have to give up pagan feasts and pagan vices. I loved my sins. The price was too high. I will not be persuaded by this Paul. I will not give up my sins. I am too fond of the life of this world to follow JESUS. I will not be persuaded. Yes, I would like to have my sins forgiven but there is too much to give up. So I said to Paul: '**Almost thou persuadest me to be a Christian**.' And Paul replied: '**I would to God, that not only thou but also all that hear me this day, were both almost and altogether such as I am except these bonds**.'

"Yes, would to GOD that I had been fully persuaded to be a Christian! Would to GOD that my tongue had burned before I had said almost! Of what avail is my position as King now? Even those who fawned on me upon earth mock and ridicule me in hell. Of what avail are my sins now? The remembrance of them sears my conscience and adds to my torment. Upon earth the things of the earth seem to be so important and of such great value. But what doth it profit a man if he gain the whole world and lose his own soul as I have done?

"Almost Heaven was mine. Almost forgiveness was mine. Almost CHRIST was mine. Almost, almost, almost. That is the flame of hell which torments me day and night. Would to GOD I had been fully persuaded to be a Christian!"

46963419R00068

Made in the USA
Lexington, KY
21 November 2015